OFF THE GRID

Off the Grid

Off the Grid

Modern Homes + Alternative Energy   Lori Ryker

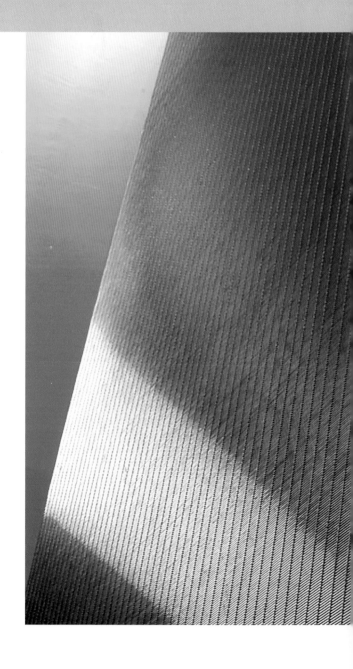

Gibbs Smith, Publisher
To Enrich and Inspire Humankind

WITHDRAWN

First Edition
09 08 07 06 05   5 4 3 2 1

Published by
Gibbs Smith, Publisher
P.O. Box 667
Layton, Utah 84041

Orders: 1.800.748.5439
www.gibbs-smith.com
Designed by Wright Design
Printed and bound in Hong Kong

Library of Congress Cataloging-in-Publication Data

Ryker, Lori, 1963–
    Off the grid : modern homes + alternative energy / Lori
Ryker.—1st ed.
        p. cm.
    Includes bibliographical references and index.
    ISBN 1-58685-516-6
  1. Architecture, Domestic—Environmental aspects. 2.
Architecture and energy conservation.   I. Title.

NA7117.3.R97 2005
728'.370472—dc22

                            2005010478

Contents

Introduction

This book provides an introduction to the concepts, techniques, and application of environmentally resourceful energy strategies. It is a "think" book for those who are interested in understanding the basics of off-the-grid energy and its potential applications.

The projects included in this book were inspired by each homeowner's desire to live in a less-resource-reliant home. The result of this desire is the creation of architecture developed out of collaboration among the client, architect, builder, and technical supplier. Although these ideas for off-the-grid energy sources are not new, their best application can seem overwhelming to the client and the uninitiated architect or designer. The profiles within this book represent ten of the design world's groundbreaking projects and individuals who are personally committed to creating ecologically balanced homes that exist in greater harmony with their surroundings than has occurred thus far in the modern era.

The architects and designers whose work is represented here are committed to finding the best-suited alternative energy strategies for a home's design and location, always keeping in mind the beauty of the home. Each house's energy source or sources is also integrated with additional practices for creating a sustainable home.

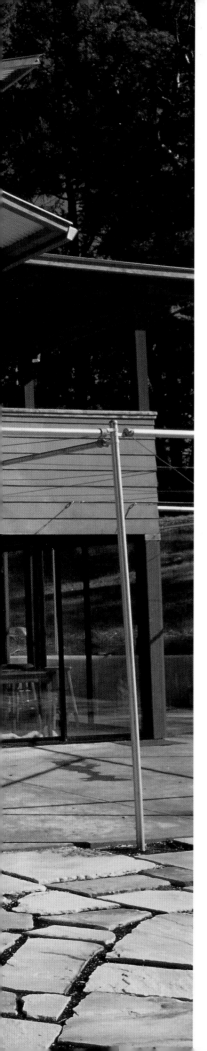

The Grid Intertie:

The Interconnection of Western Civilization

An almost-invisible grid of infrastructure binds us together. It is a system of electrical poles, wire, and substations, with hydroelectric dams and tele-communication towers, webs of highways, and systems of sewage and water extraction from both free-flowing and dammed sources. From within this system we work and play, raise families, and grow old. From within this infrastructure we also have come to one of the greatest environmental challenges known to modern civilization. The signs of our impact upon the world can be recognized in the reports of environmental and global changes occurring across the earth. They can also be seen in the growing number of energy grid failures across the world, as the system we have created is stressed beyond its capacity.

The technological advances of Western civilization's past two hundred years have provided great changes in how life is lived. In the time it took our great-grandparents' grandparents to emigrate from Europe to the United States and send their children out west, we have invented and built a grid infrastructure of energy and supply that ties us to the modernized civilization of the twenty-first century. It also leaves us responsible to a world that is struggling to survive amid the by-products of our own advantages.

In the past two hundred years Western civilization has experienced rapid changes in the quality of life created by an infrastructure that disappears seamlessly into our day-to-day lives. It is the seamlessness of these opportunities that makes their consequences difficult to come to terms with. When William Murdock invented the coal gaslight in 1792, it would have been difficult to foresee that it would later be part of the coal pollution that coated cities and rural land-scapes alike with soot. While the gaslight marked the beginning of a great environmental change, within forty years the launch of modernized and mechanized industries using a similar technique created a by-product of toxic coal pools that no one knew how to deal with. Developing industries created unhealthy conditions, from smog to contaminated drinking water, which were further exacerbated by the increase of population in the cities as people migrated to fill the new jobs created by the industries themselves. It appeared that for every new technology created, a new condition of pollution and its effects arose.

These first lessons of industrialization and pollution brought promises of cleaner environments in the form of developing municipal systems. The primary level of infrastructure was the sewer system, which was hidden below the public ways of the growing cities. The development of these waste ways at the beginning of the nineteenth century helped to rid cities of open sewers running through the streets. The sewer system dealt with the stench for which cities had become known, but also, by separating the public from such conditions, produced less disease and a healthier population.

Infrastructure continued to evolve and by 1840, railroad lines across the United States were allowing expansion across the landscape at an unprecedented rate. As populations moved into the Midwest, industry moved with them and, along with locomotive steam engines fired by coal, released the beginning of a new era of pollution into otherwise-clean air.

The late 1800s were a time of great experimental production. Machine invention was seen as a demonstration of America's potential within the context of expanding Western civilization. In 1876 the telephone, a great implementation of communication, was invented by Alexander Bell. However, in order for the technology to reach the masses, an infrastructure of wires was required across all lands. In the United States, the infrastructure was supported by the copper mines of Butte, Montana.

In the same period Thomas Edison invented the lightbulb, and it took only a few years for power lines and stations to spread like a spiderweb across the Western landscape. Now, for the first time, the grid of industrialization was apparent for all to see. As roadways were built over common paths, routes were established through countryside and city alike.

Henry Ford developed a successful system of mass production in 1913 and the automobile became a common site on the expanding roadways. Often rail, roadway, power, and telephone followed the same route as the grid expanded, effortlessly incorporating into our evolving cultural context. Perhaps it was this observable infrastructure and its potential impact upon the world that prompted German physician Ernst Haeckel, in 1866, to coin the term *ecology*, the study of the interrelations of organisms and their environments.

In the early 1900s, homes in cities and towns across America were heated by coal brought in from the mines of the rural countryside. The typical heating system found in most houses was pressure-heated water run through pipes and radiators. Soon after, the growing coal and natural gas industries recognized that they could ease individual homeowner's burden of constant maintenance of their coal furnaces while extending their own profit through the organization of large cooperatives and hubs that generated the energy out of the home. Coal-burning furnaces were removed and retrofitted to allow for the direct and seamless entry of gas into home systems, all the while contributing another system of infrastructure to the grid of modern living. Coal burning, relegated to remote locations out of the sight and experience of most city dwellers, was used to generate energy that was translated into electrical power.

Hydropower is one of the most ancient energy sources and was used to power such things as Greek and Roman baths and gristmills. In the modern era, it was reinvented in combination with modern dams. Using the force of water collected behind a dam with controlled outlets resulted in a new energy source. The first modern hydropower dam was put into service in 1830, in Appleton, Wisconsin. Since that time dams small and large, built for the creation of energy, have been altering rivers throughout rural areas, changing forever the environments the rivers moved through for thousands of years.

Clean water was piped into homes through an infrastructure similar to the one that removed sewage. Such a system seems a simple enough idea today, but it was quite a luxury at the time. Some locales were fortunate enough to have rivers, lakes, or springs nearby. For others, water was more difficult to come by and reservoirs or dams were built to retain water for expanding urban environments. In arid places, such as southern California and Arizona, water was almost nonexistent. Billions of dollars were spent to divert the Colorado River through large canals, making the West a desirable place to live but draining life from one of its native waterways.

In a period of approximately one hundred years, the average American household moved from the outhouse to the bathroom, complete with indoor plumbing and shower; from the constant vigil of a coal furnace, wood-burning stove, or fireplace to the turn of a lever to take the chill off; from gas lantern to a constant glow of lumens; from the hand pump out back to sink and shower faucets that not only produced water at the turn of the knob, but allowed you to moderate the temperature of the water from hot to cold. The grid of infrastructure we seldom recognize or question completely modernized our way of life.

These advances brought great times. Conveniences abounded. In fact, convenience became the operative and active concept for Western civilization's cultural evolution. Most of the Western world benefited from the inventions of what became known as "the grid of infrastructure" in built environments of all sizes. Even rural residences saw great benefit as electrified copper conduit was strung out along poles and dropped right into their homes; electricity not only lit homes, but it also powered the pumps for wells, bringing water into the farmhouse. Propane gas was developed for holding tanks in order to provide a similar heating system that the city dweller reveled in, and highway systems and rail lines brought the newest technologies to the local mercantile.

What we didn't recognize at the time was the negative consequence of such modernizations. Environmental destruction and devastation that would only later be recognized for its full global impact occurred at scales small and large. Within the same amount of time that we created lives of convenience on the grid, we contributed a wasteland of by-products from our convenient lifestyle for which we gave little forethought.

We can recognize the effects of our lifestyle through the example left us Berkeley Pit in Butte, Montana. The copper wire that connected power and phone from the East to the West Coast was mined in Butte, Montana, which resulted in the largest EPA Super Fund clean-up site in the United States, and one of the most polluted environments in the world. The toxic water from the mining process has polluted the local water supply and surface water, including the infamous Clark Fork River that eventually drains into the Columbia River. The water that rises inside the pit is so toxic that when, in 1995, a flock of more than three

hundred Canada geese landed on the water during migration, they died overnight. The Glen Canyon dam, completed in 1963, provides another example of unforeseen environmental pollution. The damming of the Colorado River for a reservoir and energy generation resulted in the then second-largest artificial lake in the United States. It is currently filling with toxic pollution and sediment, bringing the pros and cons of an appropriate solution to its energy contributions and wildlife hazards into heated debate.

Coal, gas, and oil have left their mark in the atmosphere in the form of a deteriorating ozone layer, acid rain, greenhouse gases, and global warming. The coal-burning industry has left mountains of slag, with little or no plan for its use or reincorporation back into the environment. Some of these slag mountains are toxic themselves. Although great efforts to clean up waterways have been underway for the past few generations, our continued dumping of sewage and industrial wastewater into clean water sources brings such practices into question. The grid of infrastructure we live with every day brings a more-polluted environment and dwindling, nonrenewable energy sources with results that are both obvious and obscured.

We cannot wholly blame the industries and corporations for the polluted landscape with which we are left because we happily accepted the conveniences they offered. But we can take responsibility for our future choices and conveniences today. We can recognize that we are part of a larger place than the city, town, or rural area in which we live; we are part of an environment that extends to include a complex biological system we are only beginning to understand. We are also living in an era when we can employ new technological innovations that have less impact on the environment, are safer and healthier for everyone, and promise to safeguard a future for our descendants and the life that extends beyond our front doors.

By drawing from ancient concepts of living, simple energy concepts, and advanced technological interpretations of these concepts, we have the opportunity to incorporate cleaner energy supplies into our lives. The popularized term for these systems is "off the grid." It is a term that simply refers to systems that work independently from the larger municipal systems. They are systems that

can be monitored by a homeowner to ensure that the water or energy they use does not contribute to environmental pollution and degradation. These systems also offer options to ensure that the removal of waste from the home contributes as little as possible to the pollution in our water, air, and ground.

The homes presented in this book, each in varying ways, incorporate the "off the grid" concept. Whether urban, suburban, or rural, each homeowner has taken the health of the environment as his or her own responsibility. In both small and large ways, techniques of environmental conservation and clean energy are incorporated as budgets and locale allow. What this book aims to make clear is that living off the grid is a concept that can be easily understood and adopted by everyone, regardless of where you live or how much money you make. The homes presented here demonstrate that choices for a healthier world can come together with the aspirations of great designs, and that the infrastructure for living begun two hundred years ago may be transformed into a new system that is based on our knowledge of the interconnected and fragile world to which we belong.

Sustainable Living and Off-the-Grid Technologies

Creating sustainable living environments involves rethinking four separate elements: materials of construction, passive (or nonmechanized) energy strategies, active (or mechanized) energy systems, and the synthesis of the design into a beautiful and environmentally integrated experience. While the idea of sustainable living has been explored and implemented by professional architects, designers, and builders over the past quarter of a century, most considerations focus on the materials of construction and passive systems, neither of which require a dramatic change in how we live. There is a simple reason for this focus: materials are a necessity of building and passive systems are an inexpensive benefit gained through thoughtful design. Active energy systems, on the other hand, are a developing group of technologies that often require greater financial commitment from the owners and a rethinking of how they might live their lives in order to save energy and resources. For most people considering an alternative energy system, the understanding of and commitment to lifestyle changes is already recognized and in simple ways implemented, such as using highly efficient lightbulbs or energy-efficient appliances. However, for most of us, finances are limited and, in the instance of energy systems, we must learn to do more with less to bring about an off-the-grid lifestyle.

The off-the-grid home and its systems is best understood when reviewed holistically. Exploring the techniques and technologies discussed in this book relative to each home and its specific objectives will help you recognize the creative and sustainable potential of your interests. The considerations and technical options employed in these alternative energy homes will also help you understand more easily each system's potential and how the different aspects work together. In an effort to make the qualities and strategies of each of the homes comprehensible, the various concepts, techniques, and design considerations used in creating an off-the-grid house are described in the next section.

The Relationship Between Passive and Active Systems

Most off-the-grid energy systems work in tandem with passive strategies. The combined efforts of passive and active strategies provide related benefits. First, a well-designed passive home can greatly reduce the energy required to heat and cool it or provide water for its operation. As a consequence, the better a passive set of strategies works within the design of a home, the less active energy systems are required. This simple fact can reduce the cost of the system, the amount of resources used to build the system, and minimize the visual impact of many systems. Additionally, this combined strategy makes us more aware of the place in which we live, and how we live in it. The simple passive concept of well-placed, operable windows allows us to recognize the changing of seasons when we open and shut them to provide adequate ventilation and cooling in our home. The breeze that moves through the windows into the house brings in the outdoor air, flushing the air inside and providing our senses a multitude of scents—from rain and plants to autumn's damp earth.

Selecting Your Energy Systems

Selecting the appropriate energy system is a decision that should be based on three factors: first, the location of the home, both its general geographic location and its particular site conditions. The general environmental conditions where you live affect the requirements for creating and maintaining a comfortable living environment and your experience of the home environment. For example, if you live in a place with high precipitation you could collect rainwater for your home's use, and the method of the collection, such as along gutters and rain chains, can accentuate the beauty and experience of how and where you live. The second factor is budget. Understanding your desired goals and how they may be attained with your available finances is critical to the holistic design of your system. The third factor is learning about the legal conditions and requirements for implementing off-the-grid systems in your community.

Understanding Your Environment, Understanding Where You Live

Many of the valuable strategies from premodern or vernacular buildings demonstrate the "common sense" qualities of building that were pushed aside as we made advances in technology. One example of how an environment helped to shape a vernacular building form is found in the southern part of the United States. This climate has long, hot, humid summers and mild winters. As a way to remain as cool as possible in the extreme weather of summer, porches with deep overhangs for shade were adopted. This allowed the air to cool before it entered the house. Another strategy used was to break a building's components into parts with breezeways in between, which funneled the cooled air through the structures while outdoor rooms were created in the breezeways.

As nonrenewable energy sources are becoming scarce and the majority of the methods of their extraction are damaging to the health and quality of the environment, simple passive strategies for creating comfortable environments are once again being applied. Such strategies are timeless and always applicable to a specific environment to make places for comfortable living.

Additionally, passive strategies reduce the overall energy required to heat and cool a home or to heat and cool water. This fact cannot be overstressed because these design aspects can have a huge impact upon the size of a photovoltaic solar array or the amount of energy you require from the municipal system in a grid-intertie program. Modifying the temperature of a well-designed home can be as simple as opening or closing a series of windows or including a "heat sink," or thermal mass, in an area of the home that will receive a lot of sunlight. This latter design consideration, which is typically incorporated through the use of concrete or concrete block, stores heat during the day and then radiates it back into the closed room at night. Simple solar hot water heaters are situated to be in contact with the sun's rays in moderate- to hot-weather environments, and can directly produce hot water for the shower with little additional technology.

There is a great experiential benefit to the passively designed home in that the minor modifications we make to our living environment, such as opening a window or drawing a shade, can help tie us to a place and time. These experiences can help us recognize that the season is changing or sense that a rainstorm is on the way. These conditions and choices for living bring us closer to where we live, making us more involved in how we live.

Understanding Appropriate Energy Sources for Your Environment

Before choosing an energy production system it is best to observe the phenomena and geographic conditions of your home. These observations, as will be recognized by any good designer or architect, will also affect the placement and design of the home. The end result will make for a more efficient system and a more responsive home. The homes in this book illustrate how designs and technologies are applied in environment-specific ways. For instance, the Barsotti residence (page 54) takes advantage of its south-oriented site by opening the southern side of the home to the sun. Its large windowed door can be opened to bring in the sun's warmth on cool but sunny days, warming the home's concrete slab and reducing the amount of energy required to heat the radiant floor. A photovoltaic array is used in this home because the region receives a high amount of sun. The Hill Country Jacal house (page 88), located in hot and humid Texas, employs deep overhangs over the living space that block the sun

but allow the southern breezes to cool the space. The large amounts of rain in this area of Texas make water collection a simple and productive strategy. A pergola along the southern face of the Fargo and Maestas residence (page 76) blocks the high summer sun while allowing the low winter sun to enter the home. A hybrid photovoltaic and wind turbine system takes advantage of the variable weather conditions of an environment that is sunny and breezy most of the year with occasional extreme weather in the winter. Lindsay Johnston's Four Horizons Autonomous House (page 142) is fully engaged in its environment, relying on its orientation for blocking winter winds and summer sun, while also providing breathtaking views into the landscape. Consideration of the forest that surrounds the house and of potential wildfires influenced the choice of construction materials and also inspired a practice of firewood gathering around the home, which reduces the potential for quick-spreading wildfires. Heavy rain seasons are counted on and taken advantage of in a series of roof-collection systems and cisterns for home, garden, and firefighting use.

The diagrams associated with each project should also aid you in interpreting the more general conditions of each project's environment. In turn, such interpretations can help you begin to develop an understanding of the potential conditions where you live: which direction summer and winter breezes come from, the amount of rain that falls in a year, and the degree of humidity in the air. All of these can affect passive and active energy potential.

Practicalities

Financial Commitment

With all off-the-grid energy and resource technologies the major cost of the system is upfront. This is different from grid-tied systems where you pay for the use of the system month by month in a never-ending bill cycle. Off-the-grid systems require one-time payments, with some minor maintenance costs. For this reason such systems are more expensive initially, but at some point in their use they are fully paid for when compared with costs of the conventional grid system payment and inflation of services over the years. The relation between the initial cost of systems and their "payoff" period varies depending on the initial cost of the system, its type, and degree of use. For instance, a hot-water solar panel may pay for itself in a year, while a photovoltaic array may not pay for itself for ten years or more.

Rebates

Rebates for energy-efficient and alternative technologies are often offered at city and state levels. You can find out what rebates are available where you live by contacting the city directly, talking to the permitting offices, or reviewing their Web sites.

The Legal Issues

Each political entity—city, county, and state—will have its own regulations for implementing various off-the-grid technologies. It is important to discuss these regulations with your architect and technical support provider before committing to a particular technology.

Maintenance of the System

All systems require upkeep. However, some require less than others. When exploring potential systems it is important to discuss your home's maintenance with your architect and technical provider. While some systems require upkeep, such as keeping the filter in a hydro turbine clean, the effort can be worth the outcome because a hydro turbine can be one of the most cost-effective off-the-grid technologies to employ. It is important to match the upkeep requirements of your system with your style of life.

Insulation

Proper and appropriate insulation is a necessity for the efficient use of energy and technologies. This is an important condition to remember when developing a new home with alternative energy or adding systems to an existing home. While there are government standards for wall and roof insulation, providing greater insulated conditions for the home will only help reduce the energy required to heat or cool it. In addition, in the past several years better insulators that are also better for the environment have come into production. Icynene, recycled denim-fiber batts, and formaldehyde-free batts with recycled-glass content all provide great insulative value and are better for the environment than conventional fiberglass batting or sprayed polyurethane insulation.

Completely Off the Grid or Grid Intertied: A Working Concept

Off the Grid

The degree of independence from the grid that you achieve most often depends which region of the country you live in and your budget. Other primary factors include whether you live in a city or rural environment, the local climactic conditions, your initial financial commitment, and even your commitment of generosity to your neighbors and the health of the planet.

When hearing the phrase *off the grid,* most of us imagine a home that lies in a rural location with no reliance on the general grid-tied energy sources. However, when you understand that there are many technologies that provide options for living in varied stages of energy conservation relative to our reliance on conventional energy sources, you begin to recognize a more accurate description of these technologies. *Off the grid* is a term that best describes strategies and technologies of alternative energy systems, rather than a home that operates without any external energy inputs.

While your goal may be to live 100 percent free of municipal energy systems, your budget may require that this goal be achieved over a period of time. Living a resource-conservative lifestyle, while not completely off the grid, is a beneficial step for everyone and the planet.

Grid Intertie

Grid intertie refers to a system that incorporates off-the-grid technologies while remaining connected to municipal systems. Such a strategy is adopted for a number of reasons. The most common is the inability to fully provide energy requirements from alternative energy sources, when a grid tie is possible. Other common reasons are that the home is already connected to the municipal systems, the home is within the city limits, or the alternative systems are only permitted if the homeowner participates in a buyback program that sells extra energy to the municipal grid. A grid intertie may involve a combined energy strategy such as independence from the grid for electrical power but reliance for water, or an independence for gas but not sewer.

In both semirural and community locations the grid supply may already be located at the property line. This condition provides an opportunity to choose the technology and the amount of energy obtained from the technology. You might introduce a small photovoltaic panel to provide the energy for a specific energy requirement, such as heat, or to reduce your overall grid energy draw. Or if you live within the domain of an energy supplier who has a buyback program you may elect to work from a grid-intertie system. In such a system the energy you produce, 100 percent or less, is used by your residence first, then "sold" or credited back to the local energy provider for them to sell to your neighbors. In the instance that you require additional energy, the power company supplies you that energy directly. Energy companies use a variety of contracts and it is important to understand how a contract works if you choose a grid-intertie buyback system. Some companies offer rebate incentives to residences that choose a grid intertie because it decreases the amount of energy the company needs to produce. There is a less obvious benefit to returning energy back to the grid: the energy you produce will be sent directly to your neighbors, benefiting your local environment. If you manage to produce more than 100 percent of your energy requirements at particular times of the year, you are providing a contribution to the health of the planet.

You may also elect to run one of your utility sources fully off the grid, while other utilities remain tied to the community source. For instance, you might employ a photovoltaic array for all of your electrical power while using a municipal supply of natural gas. This source might supply all of your general electricity to run your appliances, while natural gas may come directly from the utility company and supply energy for your water heater or gas range.

Many people interested in alternative energy and utility resources cannot afford to be fully off the grid. If your goal for incorporating alternative and off-the-grid energy sources is based on reducing your reliance on resource extraction and "dirty" energy, choosing which alternative energy strategy to employ should be made only after you've considered the total energy requirements for your home and each potential source's ability to create the cleanest energy or potential energy in the future. You might start with a simple photovoltaic system and prepare the home for the later addition of a solar water heater.

The Technologies

Because off-the-grid systems are intimately tied to the environmental conditions that energize them, the different technologies shown here are categorized by the elements of earth, wind, sun, and water.

Earth

We often think of earth as the inert mass of the planet. However, earth is a dynamic element that evolves, most often at a slower rate than other aspects of our planet. Like our atmosphere, we must consider what we remove from the ground as well as what we put into it. We have a great impact upon our own health and the planet's health when we choose our energy sources. The greatest extraction of resources for energy is coal—from coal-bed methane to natural gas—removed from the earth with lasting environmental consequences. However, earth also offers a more benign option for our energy needs.

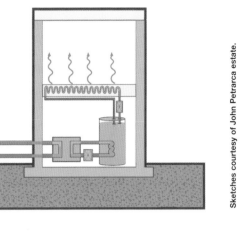

Diagrams showing geothermal heating and cooling systems, as used in Reade Street Townhouse (see page 110).

Geothermal Energy

Geothermal strategies have been used for thousands of years to heat and cool our shelters. The concept is simple. While the earth's surface temperature fluctuates with the season, below the surface such temperature sways are stabilized between 45 and 70 degrees Fahrenheit. In the past, the use of this condition has been employed in passive strategies, such as building a home into a hillside, or partially submerged in the earth. In other instances a series of "ducts" were dug into the ground adjacent or below the home and the air was drawn up and into the home, with only minimal energy required to heat 50-degree air to a warmer temperature. The result was that when the air was hot outside, the air inside would be cooled from the mass of the earth, and when the outside air was cold, the inside air would be warm.

Technologically advanced systems are currently employed along with the simple, using the same concepts combined with more energy-efficient and environmentally responsive options such as a well loop. These systems can be employed anywhere the more-stable ground temperature can be tapped into. While geothermal energy is often employed in remote locations, it is not limited to these environments, and as shown in the Reade Street townhouse in New York City (page 110) and House R128 in Stuttgart (page 122), such energy-conscious options can be most appropriate to urban and semiurban conditions.

Composting Toilets

Composting toilets are most often employed in rural areas where a municipal sewage line is not offered or in semirural areas where a homeowner is interested in reducing both his/her overall use of clean water and the stress on waterways that become polluted from runoff or the dumping of sewage. A composting toilet operates as its name implies; over time, waste collected into a holding tank is changed into a composted material that may be returned to the ground as a benign and valuable soil additive. The systems available can be low tech or more advanced depending on the overall use and long-term intent for the waste. The required maintenance of the different systems ranges in needs from regularly using a biodegradable additive to a yearly cleaning of virtually maintenance-free systems. In some instances toilets are linked together to a larger composting vat that also serves as composting for all the home's biodegradable refuse. The minimized use of water in a composting toilet means a home's amount of created gray water is reduced. A reduction in gray water means there is less by-product from our lives requiring action and responsibility.

The composting toilet is a very safe system for the environment, but while it remains a well-known system, it is not employed to its fullest potential. The chief reason for this appears to be that, in many municipalities, composting toilets are either not permitted as the primary toilet or not permitted at all.

Wind
Wind Turbines

Wind turbines are one of the most visually dynamic and physically active systems employed for no-emission energy production. As many large-scale wind farms are being developed across the world to support communities, there is also an increase in the number of single-family homeowners incorporating smaller systems. Wind turbines vary in size, increasing the amount of energy output relative to the home size and the potential energy used. Most domestic-scale wind turbines are 80 to 120 feet tall with blades extending to 21 feet in diameter, located on land of one acre or more. Due to the wear and tear on moving parts, wind turbines will require periodic maintenance and adjustments. Wind turbines are best used in a constant wind of at least 8 miles per hour (the Department of Energy Class 2 minimum wind resource.) Slower winds mean less energy produced. Reciprocally, wind speeds exceeding 30 miles per hour decrease the operations of the system; in effect, turbines will "shut down" in high-wind and gusty conditions. Photovoltaic systems will only produce a one-to-one energy ratio relative to their amount of cells and their exposure to the sun, but a wind turbine produces exponentially more energy relative to its increased wind speed up to 30 miles per hour. However, there are few places where the wind is as reliable as the sun. For this reason most wind turbines are combined with a photovoltaic array, with the assumption that if the wind is not blowing, the sun will typically be shining. This combination is often referred to as a wind/solar hybrid.

Sun
Photovoltaic Arrays

Photovoltaic arrays, often called solar panels or P.V.s, are viewed as the most predominant, reliable, clean energy generator available today. Their system is internal and without moving parts, making it also simple to operate. Typically, once a system is installed and in operation it requires no upkeep. These characteristics make photovoltaic arrays a popular choice with homeowners and technicians alike. There are several types of photovoltaic systems, ranging from conventional panels to advanced photovoltaic glazing systems with integrated solar cells to photovoltaic shingles and laminates that adhere to smooth surfaces.

Panel systems have been in existence the longest, and have data from which technicians can project their life spans. These systems are an assembly of cells, which, when grouped together into panels, are called an array. An array, like all alternative energy systems, is sized according to the homeowner's projected energy load's estimated consumption of kilowatt hours. The array is placed where it will receive the most direct sun for the longest number of hours each day. Often arrays are mounted on roofs where the pitch is similar to the angle required for solar gain. Mounting the array in line with the roof helps to blend the panels with the profile of the roof. An example of this installation method can be seen in the Barsotti residence (page 54) and the D'Souza and de la Torre residence (page 98). An array can also be used for its sculptural potential as is seen in the Solar

Umbrella House (page 40). In this instance the panels literally become a sun shield for the second-floor terrace. An array can also be "pole mounted," situated independently from the home, as seen in the Fargo and Maestas residence (page 76). Such a system can provide several advantages in a cold-weather environment where gaining the maximum solar gain is desirable and the roof pitch may run contrary to the desired mounting condition. A pole-mounted array can also have a mounting system that tracks the sun over the day, so as to accumulate as much solar gain as possible.

While the laminate and integrated photovoltaic systems cost more, they can be integrated more seamlessly into an architectural design, such as in vertical applications of glass windows. Their translucence allows them to be employed as a sun shield for large glass expanses. The gamble in these newer systems is in their life span: With only minimal data to date, technicians can only speculate how long the system will last.

In locations where energy is generated solely through alternative technology, photovoltaic arrays are often coupled with wind turbines, micro hydro turbines, or solar water heaters. These hybrid systems can result in fully off-the-grid energy production as can be seen in the Fargo and Maestas residence (page 76).

Solar Water Heaters

Solar hot water heaters rely on the energy of the sun for their power, but water is the method of energy transfer. The concept of the system is simple: Tubes held within a reflective panel hold water or another liquid, and, when exposed to the sun, gather heat. The heat is then transferred to its intended use, such as heating a floor or heating a hot-water tank through a coil system. In milder climates the water of a solar water system can be used directly as a hot-water source for bathing or radiant heat. Often these systems are used to bring water to a warmer degree than would come out of the ground or municipal system, reducing the amount of energy required to heat water to the desired temperature. Such systems can also be used in conjunction with photovoltaic arrays when the array is the energy source used to boost the water to its final and usable temperature. In colder climates the solar water-heating system does not have water running through it, but a substitute called glycol. Glycol does not freeze in cold weather so it can be employed as an energy transmitter, pumped through a radiant floor system or to the hot-water system in an internalized coil.

Water

Micro Hydropower

Micro hydropower is one of the oldest energy-producing technologies still in use today. Power-generating turbines come in a variety of scales. The hydro generator, like the photovoltaic array, is one of the most reliable sources for generating energy. The system's requirements are determined based on running water and its relation of head (the height between the source intake and turbine) and amount of water flow. A water source may have a large head and less water flow, or it may have less head and more water flow and still produce the same amount of energy. Micro hydropower systems can be set in small creeks with intakes and holders or diverters that then allow the water to continue through its course with minimal impact. This system is referred to as a "run of river." Today, many systems are being reintroduced in homes and lodges where water flows twelve months of the year. A difference between hydro and wind or solar power is that the size of the hydro system is limited to the energy source in a one-time use condition, while solar and wind turbines can be added to, as long as there is space for them.

Rainwater Collection and Reclamation

Rainwater or snowmelt collection can be developed as a sophisticated program for providing water for an entire home, or a simple one that provides water for a garden. The potential for the system depends on the environment and goals of the homeowner. The most common method of rainwater collection is from a roof into a storage tank, or cistern. Environment plays a role in the system's success, because while rainwater collection may be desirable, if you live in a place where it doesn't rain often, or you have minimal roof surface, only minor amounts of water can be collected. Texas and Florida, for instance, are ideal environments for collecting rainwater for an entire home, while homes in desert environments are typically at a disadvantage. A successful system requires a well-designed roof and gutter system and filtering system to clean the water for the desired use. Some systems are installed to use nonfiltered water, or water that you do not intend to drink, for needs like toilets or washing clothes. More sophisticated filtering systems can be employed if the water is intended for consumption. However, the more sophisticated the filtering system, the more room is required to house both it and the storage tanks that will hold the initially collected and the filtered water. These systems require a pump with the cistern or storage tank so that the water is available on demand. The Hill Country Jacal house in Texas (page 88) illustrates a simple storage system.

While home-use water collection requires a well-designed system, a small rainwater collection system can be developed with a more ad hoc system of above-ground containers arranged to gravity feed gardens and landscape. In either application, groundwater use is reduced.

Gray Water Collection and Reclamation

Another water-conserving system is gray water collection and reclamation. Gray water, as was mentioned earlier, is water that is nonpotable. In this instance gray water refers to any water, except toilet water, within the home that has already been used once, but with minimal effort could be used again for another purpose before being released from the home. For example, water from the shower or washing machine can be piped within the home to be stored and routed into the toilets for flushing, or it can be stored and with minimal filtering be used for the landscape. Toilet/sink combinations also exist in which the water first runs through the sink and then is stored in the toilet tank for later flushing. It is important to remember that gray water that is minimally filtered must have only biodegradable soaps in it.

Living Machines and Constructed Wetlands

Gray water can be filtered through a sophisticated system called a "living machine" in which all gray or used water is run through a series of biotic filters that purify the water so that it is clean enough to drink. Living machines are miniature wetlands housed inside. Developed by Dr. John Todd, this system is used not only in private residences but also in public buildings throughout the world. The living machine creates a closed-loop system where very little additional water is required because of its efficiency.

Constructed wetlands are another form of gray water reclamation. In these systems, concepts similar to the living machine are employed. The goal of a man-made wetland is to replicate a natural wetland's ability to clean and filter water. A constructed wetland system's selected plants filter gray water in a specific order, and then return the water to the earth, eliminating the need for a fully developed septic system.

Fire
Fireplaces and Woodstoves

Wood-burning or pellet-burning systems are a simple and obvious choice for small homes that require off-the-grid heating. They are also, of course, one of the most ancient technologies and are heavily tied to our roots of domesticity, ritual, and shelter. For this reason, fireplaces have survived despite their reduced energy efficiency. Even though they are often unable to heat large spaces or store and project heat, and they contribute pollution to the environment, a fireplace's ability to help return us to a more primal state of mind provides beneficial experiences that cannot be denied. You can plan for and design fire-burning systems that are the most applicable to the environment in which they will be employed and as energy efficient as possible. David Buege's Twin Lakes cabin (page 64) is an excellent example of the appropriate use of a wood-burning stove. This small cabin is not in use full time, negating the need for a more expensive energy system. The cabin's size also allows for the stove to fully heat the cabin; a fire built during the evening keeps the cabin warm through the entire night with no additional wood. This only works in a well-built, well-insulated structure. Also, the cabin's location in remote Minnesotan woods allows for the collection of firewood from the forest floor. The Barsotti residence (page 54) with its multiple fireplaces in the same masonry core, was designed so the core would heat up and warm the entire two-story space. In addition, one of the fireplaces serves as a cooking oven, creating a dual use for the fire. The Wilson residence (page 132) with its small wood-burning stove and internal flue exposed through the second-story space, also heats both the lower and upper floors.

Backup, Batteries, and Inverters
Gas Generators

Gas generators are probably the most common form of off-the-grid technology. Many people experience failures from their community grid-tied power due to surges of power or storms. To prepare for these energy losses, gas generators are stored in garages or basements. In other living situations, where heat is a life-or-death condition, a gas generator is employed as a backup energy source in the instance that solar, wind, or geothermal systems cannot produce enough energy. However, using gas generators does not help decrease pollution, decrease the extraction of resources from the earth, or serve as a long-term solution. Propane/gas generators should only be used as an emergency solution. The example of generators helps us to understand how there is a broad range of strategies of energy use and implementation between grid-reliant energy and energy sourced 100 percent off the grid.

Batteries

Energy requirements for a home are a constant, but the sources for off-the-grid or alternative energy fluctuate due to environmental conditions. Due to this fact, fully off-the-grid homes employ battery banks to store energy for those times when their systems are not producing enough energy for a direct-source use between generator and activity. The size of the bank is determined by the potential factor of system downtime estimated by the technical specialist you work with. Batteries also have a life span, and their replacement will be required long before your energy system requires replacing, so in some instances it may be a better choice to work through a grid-intertie system to ensure energy availability and to reduce the need for replacement and maintenance of a battery bank.

Battery banks may also be employed in grid-intertied houses for a few other applications. In the instance that the grid energy suffers a failure, and the intertie system cannot provide all of your energy needs, a supplement will be needed (a similar situation to the gas generator). For some buyback systems, a strategy may be adopted to hold energy in batteries and then sell it back at the peak energy time to produce the greatest financial gain for your production.

Inverters

In a battery-based system, inverters are required to convert the stored DC battery power into the AC output power used by most electrical apparatuses.

From Grid Tie to Complete Independence

Successfully using the various alternative energy systems and their applications requires an understanding of how you live and how you want to live. A grid-intertie system will allow most people to live with the same high-energy-consumption experiences as their on-the-grid neighbors, but monitoring your energy use from the grid should remain a focus of the household. The value of these technologies is only fully realized when we create a less-energy-reliant lifestyle. Since most of us have lived our lives using as much energy as we want without being fully responsible for the tie between lifestyle and energy requirements, most people who desire to live off the grid will be required to change or modify their lifestyles. These changes, however, need not be looked at as sacrifices, but rather as fine-tuning. As we engage in these techniques and technologies for living in a less environmentally extractive way we also have the opportunity to become more in tune with our surroundings. We recognize the relationship between a series of overcast days and reduced energy availability and how we live. We can plan our lives with the forecast of weather and no longer live as if what is happening outside has no bearing upon how we live inside. A cool gray day may suggest that we plan on a fire in the wood-burning stove. On the other hand, days when energy is at peak production can allow us to perform heavy energy-requirement tasks such as vacuuming or doing laundry. Heavy rain in the springs can provide a full cistern and the understanding that the garden will have water for an entire summer. Bright sunny days may mean not only that the photovoltaic array is producing a high degree of power but also that the solar water heaters are producing heat constantly for hot showers. On a cool day windows can be opened to allow a fresh breeze to come through south-facing windows without sacrificing the warmth in the house.

Energy and environment are a dynamic partnership. Living in response to the place we are in allows us to participate in their cycles. As can be seen in the ten projects that follow, there are a variety of options for combining passive techniques and active technologies with our expectations and visions for living, which can bring about great living in great architecture. While these examples don't exhaust the options, they can serve as a starting point for envisioning what is possible and applicable in many different environmental conditions.

The Projects

Bungalow Remodel

Pugh and Scarpa Architects and Engineers   Solar Umbrella House   Venice, California

Lawrence Scarpa has said that "every building should address issues of sustainability." It is with this vision in mind that the Solar Umbrella House was designed. Located in Venice, California, the residence is a dynamic example of one couple's commitment to conserve resources and take responsibility for the environment in which they live. Completed in the spring of 2004, the Solar Umbrella House participates in and extends the development of modern architecture with California's sympathetic temperate environment, but goes further too, clearly demonstrating that the simple beauty of the language of modern architecture can employ off-the-grid technologies and sustainable strategies to further architectural expression.

The Facts:

House: 1,880 square feet

Technology
- A 4-kilowatt solar array provides virtually 100 percent of the electrical requirements for the residence. Purchasing discontinued solar panels with a group of people provided a break in the cost of the panels.

Dynamic Use of Energy
- A radiant-heat floor system is directly heated by the solar panels.
- An electric water heater is employed to take advantage of the solar energy.
- All general use of appliances, lighting, and basic electrical power is provided by the panels.
- A gray water reclamation system is incorporated under the house to channel rainwater for irrigating the gardens.

Other Energy
- Natural gas is provided by the municipal system and is used for the gas stove and as a backup for hot-water heating.

Materials of Interest
- Homasote paneling, a material made from recycled newspaper, is used as a finished surface on the cabinets.
- Concrete is employed as a flooring surface, acting as a heat sink for the sun.
- Oriented Strand Board (OSB), a cost-effective and responsible alternative to hardwood, serves as the primary flooring where concrete is not already in place.
- Low-VOC (volatile organic compound) paint was used to surface the walls.
- A gravel hardscape allows water runoff to percolate back into the ground rather than funnel into the sewer system.

This page: The remodeled bungalow, as viewed streetside, retains the scale of its neighbors, while the dynamic addition can be seen beyond.

Facing page: The concrete base stairs transition to folded steel, supporting the experience of moving from earth to balcony.

This page: The crisp line of the "solar umbrella" wraps the house, providing energy through the photovoltaic panels while also acting as a shading device for the second floor balcony.

Facing page: The photovoltaic panel system, as it wraps up wall and over the roof, greets guests upon first entry into the home.

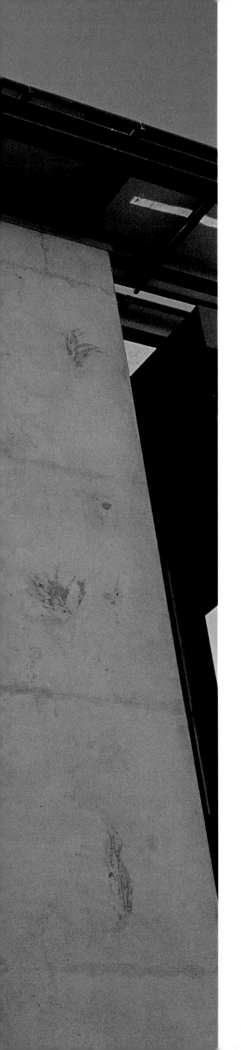

Lawrence Scarpa and Angela Brooks, the partners in charge of the Solar Umbrella House, see the embodiment of both their personal and architectural philosophies in the home's design. They "are committed to conserving the environment and intelligently utilizing the earth's natural resources," an attitude that is ever-present in the home. While the Solar Umbrella House has a sophisticated form, its expression is achieved through humble and conscientious material choices. The dynamic solar shelter, which the architects call a solar umbrella after Paul Rudolph's Umbrella House of 1953, comprises a 4-kilowatt solar panel array, which literally wraps the house from the south side, continuing up and over the roof.

The solar array acts as a screen, protecting large portions of the house from direct heat gain. It also takes in the sun's rays, accounting for an estimated 100 percent of the building's electrical energy requirements. The Solar Umbrella House's system is grid intertied, with all surplus energy returning to the municipal draw, potentially providing clean energy to the community. At the same time, should the house require more energy than the array can provide at one time, the system will reserve and temporarily provide energy to the house through its battery bank before drawing energy from the municipal grid.

This page: The dynamic relationship of space, material, texture and sculptural interplay demonstrates that off-the-grid technologies are not tied to traditional forms or types of homes.

Facing page: The pool in the courtyard, built from cast-in-place concrete, provides a dynamic and meditative element defining the path of entry from the street.

The Umbrella House is an extension of an initial remodel. Conserving the original form of the bungalow, Scarpa and Brooks took advantage of the "through lot" condition of the site, reversing the front and back of the house. This strategy allowed the house to gain its needed southern exposure for the solar array while also connecting the living area with the back garden space. The result is a contrasting expression with the dynamic entry façade of the solar array facing one street, and the more quiet and modest original structure facing the other street.

The organizing principles of the house hinge on the blurring and extension of inside to outside. Such strategies create dynamic ways to experience and incorporate the entire environment. A simple but elegant concrete swimming pool cascades along the garden's western edge, linking the outdoor garden to the house. The living room has large sliding glass doors that open out onto the garden, literally erasing the boundary of inside and out. The canopy of solar panels provides a covered space from which the garden below can be viewed from the second floor.

The Solar Umbrella House is an inspiration for environmental commitment and design and demonstrates that challenging design ideas are well suited to housing an environmentally responsible life.

This page: Viewed from the bathing area toward the master bedroom, the master suite is experienced as a whole. The head of the bed is tucked into the cabinet wall creating a niche for sleeping with views out toward the garden below.

Facing page: The master bath and bedroom incorporate a wall of storage cabinets extending from one end to the other with the floor stepping up and down, denoting zones of spatial transitions.

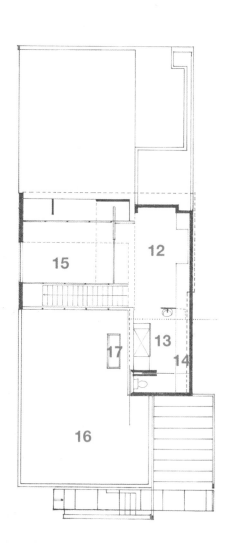

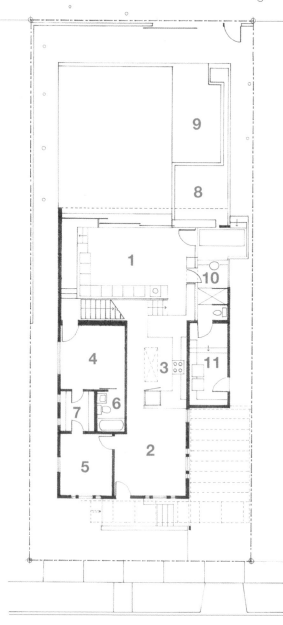

1 LIVING
2 DINING
3 KITCHEN
4 BEDROOM
5 STUDY
6 BATHROOM
7 CLOSET
8 WATER POND
9 BAMBOO PLANTER
10 BATH
11 LAUNDRY
12 MASTER BEDROOM
13 MASTER BATH
14 CLOSET
15 PATIO
16 ROOF
17 SKYLIGHT

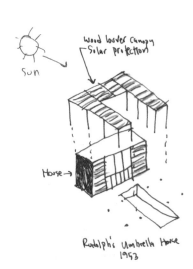

Rudolph's Umbrella House
1953

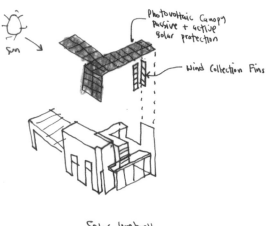

Solar Umbrella
2002

Hand drawings courtesy of Pugh + Scarpa Architects and Engineers

View from balcony, with photovoltaic "sun screen" overhead. The beauty of this project is in its poetic interpretation of the photovoltaic panels that allow us to recognize that technologies can play a dynamic part in the expression of our homes.

Above: The kitchen is connected to the outside both horizontally and vertically. A skylight painted with vibrant, low-VOC (volatile organic compound) paint, glows throughout the day and visually connects ground floor to second floor. The kitchen view extends through the living space and out into the courtyard beyond.

Facing page: Cabinetry in the kitchen is crafted from Homasote, sanded and clear-sealed. OSB (oriented strand board), a building material manufactured from remnant, compressed wood chips, serves as flooring where concrete is not employed.

Left: The ground floor cascades down stairs from the kitchen through the living area, opening out onto the courtyard through large sliding glass doors. This careful orchestration from inside to out creates a seamless living experience.

Below: Chains with weights mounted at their end guide the eye from balcony to gravel-bordered grass, a visual reminder that active water collection occurs below ground to both mitigate runoff into the street and provide water for the small garden and buffalo-grass lawn.

Indoor/Outdoor Living

Arkin/Tilt Architects   Barsotti Residence   Laytonville, California

The Barsotti residence is located in rural northern California where the beauty of the forested coastal mountains serves as both inspiration and timber supply for the surrounding communities. The home is situated in a clearing with a pond located at its southern edge. Designed to operate completely off the grid, the two-story home is organized around a south-facing courtyard and strawbale core that extends into the landscape. The extended strawbale walls orient the house in the landscape while complementing the adjacent ridge. A "light box" space serves as the primary entry at the center of the strawbale perimeter to the north. Less formal entries into the kitchen core and the passage between the front of the house and back, are to either side along the strawbale wall. The double strawbale wall provides a heavily insulated mass on the north and a gallery for the Barsottis' art collection.

The Facts:

House: 3,600 square feet

Technology
- Solar water heaters
- Photovoltaic panels from Kyocera
- Power panel inverter from Xantrex

Dynamic Use of Energy
- The radiant-heat floor system, domestic hot water, and outside patio are all directly heated by solar hot water, as will be a future hot tub.
- All electrical energy requirements are powered by the photovoltaic system.

Other Energy
- Municipal energy is available as emergency backup electricity.
- Gas-fired heat is available for emergency backup.

Materials of Interest
- The wall system is of non-load-bearing straw bales with a post-and-beam infrastructure.
- The strawbale walls have a soil-cement finish.
- Locally harvested Douglas fir, chinquapin, and redwood are used throughout.

This page: Looking across the pond, a focal point for backyard get-togethers, the profile of the mountains rising above the horizon can easily be recognized as the inspiration of the home's initial formal concept.

Facing page: A double strawbale wall entry hall serves as a gallery for the owner's art collection and provides insulation for the north side of the house.

At the owner's request the home was designed for indoor/outdoor living at least eight months out of the year. The boundary between inside and out is dissolved with the use of a large garage door that opens the living area and kitchen onto the courtyard. Deep overhangs on the home's south side provide protection from the sun in the summer but allow the low winter sun to reach inside, heating the mass of the concrete slab. At the western end of the porch the family's old bus, plugged into the home's energy sources, is still used for guests when the house is full. Passive cooling and "night flushing" are created with many operable windows and doors to the south.

Above: The bathroom, finished in reclaimed and recycled materials, is supplied with hot water by a solar water heater.

Left: Strawbale walls to the north of the living area and an open glass façade to the south heat the concrete floors and allow for efficient passive solar gain in winter months.

The variable scales of living expressed throughout the home create intimacy for two and the openness required for a crowd. Public and private space is primarily divided between the first and second floors, respectively. The living room, which lies in the center of the home, is a double-height space with a second-floor balcony connecting either side of the home. The single-story ceiling height of the kitchen and dining room, situated below the second floor, give them a more intimate scale. A rooftop dormer casts north light on a large-scale totem pole in the living area. The fireplace core, which also serves as thermal mass and fireplace to the living area, extends sculpturally up into the second floor. One fireplace faces into the kitchen and provides a wood-fired oven for cooking. Another is out of doors, facing onto the courtyard.

This page: The view from second floor balcony to living space centers on the totem pole, a gift from the owner's father, naturally daylit by a skylight. The wood ceiling and beams were built from locally harvested wood including chinquapin, redwood, and Douglas fir.

Facing page: View of the south courtyard and the exterior fireplace, which connects to the living area. The framework of the pergola will fill in with vines in the next few years, bringing the lushness of the surrounding landscape up to meet the house. The courtyard, cupped by the wings of the home on either side, helps to make a place in the larger landscape.

Left: Details incorporated into the home, such as this fossil, remind us that materials coming from the earth existed millions of years before our use of them. Such resources are not limitless and should be carefully considered for both beauty and energy effectiveness.

Facing page: Detail of south-facing overhang. The dynamic integration of knee bracing and window frames is extended to block the summer sun from entering the living area windows, keeping the interior space cool.

Below: The view from across the pond shows the entire home with its freestanding array of solar hot-water panels and "plug–in" bus guest room all blending into the landscape. Thoughtful siting strategies include the consideration of solar orientation and wind direction. Such integration with the qualities of the place not only makes for more efficient energy consumption, but also creates a more comfortable living environment.

The active energy system is a series of photovoltaic panels located on the roof of the home and a solar hot-water panel system located on the ground, set with optimal orientation for the winter months. The photovoltaic system, which provides 3.36 kilowatts of power, has a backup battery bank that allows the power to be stored and used in an emergency situation along with the home's grid intertie. The solar hot-water system serves a dual purpose: heating domestic hot water and providing the heating for the radiant floor system, which is run through a deep sand bed with concrete slab on top. Extra heat generated from this system works to heat the exterior courtyard patio and a future hot tub. Backup heat is provided by a gas-fired system.

Materials of construction were considered not only for their sustainable characteristics but also for their ability to withstand forest fire; galvanized metal was used for the roof and a soil-cement finish applied to the strawbale walls. Cement-board siding was used on the exterior walls. The interior largely incorporates locally harvested Douglas fir, chinquapin, and redwood for floors, cabinetry, and trim details.

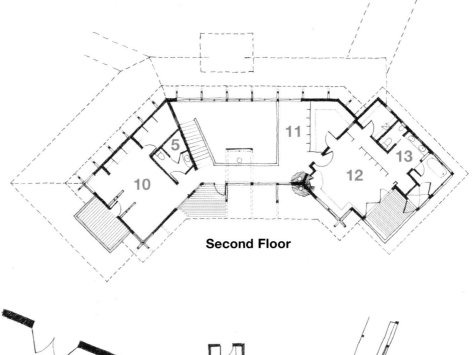

Second Floor

1 ENTRY
2 BUS PARKING
3 MEDIA ROOM
4 LIVING ROOM
5 BATHROOM
6 KITCHEN
7 LAUNDRY
8 SUN PORCH
9 SHADED COURTYARD
10 BEDROOM
11 LOFT
12 MASTER BEDROOM
13 MASTER BATH

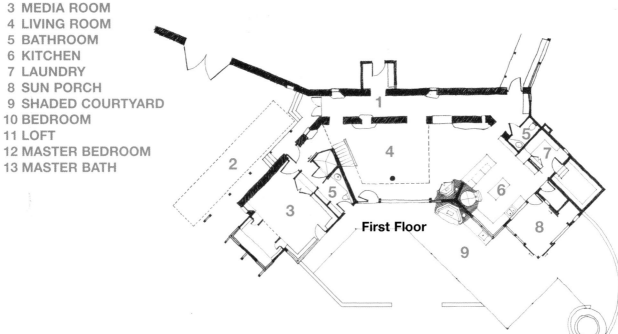

First Floor

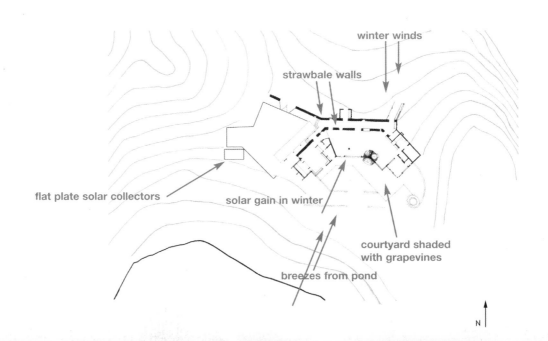

winter winds

strawbale walls

flat plate solar collectors

solar gain in winter

courtyard shaded
with grapevines

breezes from pond

N

The south-facing windows, operable garage doors, open onto the courtyard, extending living from inside to outside.

Boundary Waters Refuge

David Buege   Twin Lakes Cabin   Twin Lakes, Minnesota

Imagine the quiet smoothness of Minnesota's Boundary Waters. Your canoe paddle slips in and out of the lake, moving you closer to the cabin in the distant woods. The Twin Lakes Cabin is a family refuge far from the noises of any city or town. It is a place filled with the call of loons, the smell of wet birch leaves in fall, and the scent of pungent pine drawn out from the heat of summer's sunshine. The place is remote, both experientially and physically, from what most of us know in our daily lives. It is also fully independent from the power grid, with no option for future municipal support. Designed as a year-round retreat, the Twin Lakes Cabin sits above the lake, diminutive in size, but appropriate in scale and amenities. Without electricity, the quality of light in the cabin is directly tied to the season. Winter, when the sun is low in the sky, brings short daylight hours, while summer, when the sun is high, extends daylight until nine or ten in the evening. All year, candles provide light after dark.

The Facts:

Cabin: 348 square feet

Screen Porch: 152 square feet

Sauna: 120 square feet

Technology
- Wood stove for cabin from SCAN, Denmark
- Sauna stove from Tower, Minnesota
- Gray-water tanks for kitchen waste
- Rainwater collection for domestic cleaning

Dynamic Use of Energy
- SCAN woodstove heats the cabin in even the coldest winter weather.
- The sauna stove also heats kitchen and shower water.

Other Energy
- Two 100-pound propane tanks, refilled once a year, fuel a stove and small refrigerator.

Materials of Interest
- Insulation is reclaimed denim-fiber batts.
- The woodstove hearth is babbitt black gabbro, quarried twenty miles away.
- Kitchen counters are of greenstone slate, quarried thirty miles away.

Left: The three areas—cabin, screened porch, and sauna, each with distinct volumes—are recognizable from the woods.

Right: Large windows from the dining area provide views into the forest beyond and allow light into the cabin, both reducing the need for energy-consumptive lighting and providing passive solar heating. The loft above the dining and kitchen area varies and defines the quality of the space in the cabin; the lowered ceiling creates a comfortable area for a family meal.

With the cabin sitting on a designated "wilderness lake," all residences are required to sit 150 feet from the lakeshore. The Bueges took the wilderness qualification to heart when they designed and built the cabin, bringing all materials for construction in on a small motorboat and a pontoon boat, then walking them up the footpath to the site. The site itself was minimally cleared. As David Buege states, "We've done no clearing to open up views of the lake, preferring seclusion and obscured, or filtered, views to the water." The cabin is composed of two buildings, a living environment and a sauna, both heated by wood. In the summer and fall the cabin is opened up to the sounds, smells, and breeze of the lake. The southern side of the cabin, which is opposite to the lake view, has a large screened porch. Its location provides shelter for the porch from northwest winds, snow, and rain.

Above: A small footprint and minimal landscape destruction follows through the owner's vision of a remote cabin.

Left: View from the lake, with the cabin disappearing into the woods. The cabin's siting is informed by the community setbacks, and reminds us how we can all live with less impact on the earth, visually and ecologically.

Above: The centralized location of the wood-burning stove allows it to effectively heat the whole cabin.

Right: While more extensive and costly systems could have been employed, the remote nature of the cabin and its intermittent use call for the simplicity and straightforwardness of a traditional outhouse.

While the cabin is small, care was taken in selecting details for the interior. A small, highly efficient wood-burning stove made by SCAN of Denmark, rests on a locally quarried hearth of babbitt black gabbro. The heating system is so efficient because of walls well insulated with recycled denim scraps made into batts. The kitchen counters are made of local greenstone. A small refrigerator and stove are fueled by propane gas. Water requirements are separated between two needs, drinking and gray water; all drinking water is brought in from town, and sauna, shower, and kitchen water is brought up from the lake. The wood-fired sauna stove was made in the nearby town of Tower and serves as the heat source for shower and kitchen water. A 12-gallon water tank, secured to the side of the sauna stove, heats up the washing water and a bucket of it is used to wash off after the sauna. A bucket is also used to bring in water for the kitchen. In both the sauna and kitchen, gray-water tanks are used to retain wastewater and keep it from entering the lakes below. A simple outhouse is nearby.

The Twin Lakes Cabin, lying in the heart of some of the most pristine lake lands of the United States and Canada, offers a place of refuge for the Bueges without overextending their impact on the surrounding landscape. It is a humble structure with a quietness about it, providing exactly what is required of a retreat and nothing more.

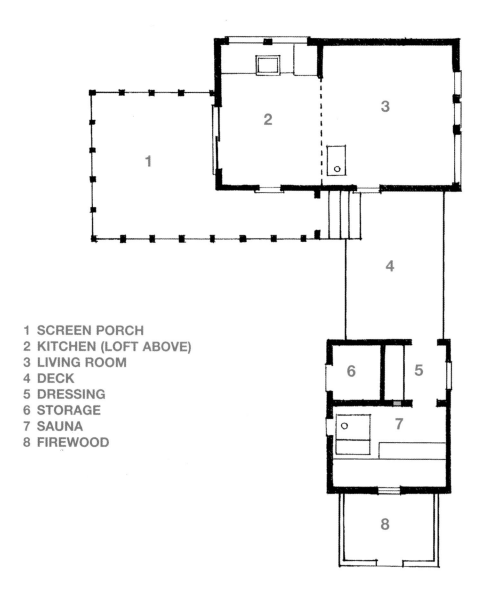

1 SCREEN PORCH
2 KITCHEN (LOFT ABOVE)
3 LIVING ROOM
4 DECK
5 DRESSING
6 STORAGE
7 SAUNA
8 FIREWOOD

The cabin and adjacent sauna create a sheltered entry into the screen porch. A simple deck serves as entry and connector to the two buildings.

Left and above: The efficiency of the cabin layout, with the kitchen tucked behind the loft ladder, provides the necessities of life for this remote cabin.

Below: The complete interior living environment can be seen here. The sleeping loft above provides a private retreat with views out through the treetops.

Above: View from the dock. The Twin Lakes Cabin is a family refuge far from modern conveniences or any large city. Visitors arrive by boat and the lifestyle is seamlessly knit to the water and woods.

Right: The large, screened porch extends living space in good weather without adding to the energy load of the cabin. Beautiful southern light filters into the porch during fall and winter, warming the space.

Below: Twin Lakes, the cabin's namesake, can be seen from inside the cabin.

Grassland Homestead

Ryker / Nave Design   Fargo and Maestas Residence   Clyde Park, Montana

The Fargo and Maestas Residence is situated in the rolling hills of the Shields Valley outside of Clyde Park in central-west Montana. From the site, four mountain ranges are visible—the Absaroka, the Crazies, the Bridgers, and Little Belt Mountains—creating breathtaking views that change with the light and season. The grassland landscape is open to the sky, and the climate is one of almost-always sunny days and a consistent light breeze.

Fargo and Maestas were interested in creating a home that would be less stressful on the environment and also conserving of natural resources. Their commitment to a holistic design strategy influenced every stage of the project, from energy system decisions to primary construction methods, and insulation to finishes.

The Facts:

House: 2,866 square feet

Future studio: 908 square feet

Technology
- A Shell SP70 photovoltaic system provides 1,680 watts DC.
- Southwest Wind Power wind turbine provides 3,000 watts in 28-mph wind.
- A backup generator from Kohler has a 5,000-watt capacity.
- A battery system holds two to three day's worth of energy storage. Additional batteries could be added to take full advantage of wind output.
- Site-drilled well provides domestic water.
- A conventional septic system was installed.
- Water is collected from the roof for landscape use.
- Propane supplies energy for a boiler and water heaters.
- A future studio will be heated with a wood-burning stove.

Dynamic Use of Energy
- A radiant-heat floor system in the concrete slab is also used as a heat sink for passive sun collection in winter and for retaining a cool temperature in summer.

Materials of Interest
- Straw bales are used in infill system.
- Denim insulation is used in the ceiling and conventional wood-framed walls.
- Naturally pigmented plaster and stucco is used on strawbale surfaces.

This page: A low-profile, cold-rolled, corrugated steel, which will rust with age, was used on the roofs to blend the house into the surrounding grassland landscape.

Facing page: The south-facing deck provides views out to the surrounding Absaroka Mountains and is oriented to the summer breezes for passive cooling in the summer.

Montana seasons are an exercise in extremes, bringing strong winds, snow, and below-freezing temperatures in winter, and strong, hot sun throughout the long daylight hours in the summer. But such conditions are a benefit when you are relying on the elements for energy. Fargo and Maestas's vision echoed the heritage of Montana's ranchers and farmers; they wanted to create their home through a type of homesteading, building it themselves. With the construction expertise of Ryker/Nave Design and the carpentry skills of Jason Cipriani, Fargo and Maestas had a resource for reference and advice during the construction process.

The result is a home that lies low across the grassy landscape, with a freestanding solar array and wind turbine oriented to take in the greatest amount of sun and wind throughout the year. The freestanding system provides an advantage for energy collection, and with the array and turbine acting as sculptural figures on the landscape, it also heightens the community's awareness of the technologies employed in the house.

Above: Two successful passive energy strategies are recognizable in the southern façade of the house. Large operable windows provide winter passive solar gain for the living room, dining room, and kitchen. In the summer the sun will be mitigated with a willow-branch-covered pergola extending from inside to out. The strawbale-walled bedrooms moderate the temperature during extreme weather swings throughout the year.

Left: In the winter, the living area receives ample sunlight for passive solar heating. The concrete slab, which also has a radiant-heat floor system, acts as a heat sink during the winter, storing the sun's heat and releasing it back into the house at night.

Fargo and Maestas, both raised in the Southwest, brought the love of thick walls with them into the Montana landscape. Ryker/Nave translated this vision into a strawbale hybrid system that incorporates a three-layer construction method of concrete, straw bales, and stud framing. This technique takes advantage of the southern sun exposure and provides heavy insulation to the north to guard against the strong winter winds. The house is set into the hill with concrete retaining walls, which reduces the home's profile toward the north and takes advantage of the insulative properties of the earth. The strawbale northern, eastern, and western walls rise out of the ground, providing insulation and expression. In this home, straw bales are used as an infill in a structural stud frame, while a conventional six-inch, wood-framed wall with denim batt insulation is used to the south. The wood-frame system allows larger expanses of glass for passive heating and southerly views toward the Absaroka Mountains.

The strawbale system also creates highly insulated volumes in the bedrooms, keeping the rooms warm in winter and cool in the summer. A passive strategy incorporating the sun and summer breezes from the south is employed in the primary living space, including the kitchen, dining, and living area. Along the southern wall multiple sets of double-glazed doors and operable windows open out onto a series of decks with pergolas. The pergolas, covered with willow branches, shelter the deck and guard the southern windows from the strong, high summer sun. The covered deck also allows living to expand outside in the spring, summer, and fall. In the winter, as the sun lies low in the sky, the sun reaches deep into the rooms, allowing the concrete floors in the living area and master bedroom to perform as a heat sink. A fireplace, with internal flue, provides additional heat in the winter. In the extreme winter months a radiant-heat floor system powered by propane provides efficient heat.

This page: Viewed from the exterior, the strawbale-infill walls finished with stucco below and thinner, stud-framed walls above, articulate the horizontal nature of the home in the surrounding grassland. A neutral material palette was selected to blend the house with the colors found in the landscape.

Facing page: A bedroom's hybrid strawbale-infill and stud-frame wall is visibly expressed. This wall system, typical of all strawbale wall systems, moderates the home's temperature from the exterior temperatures, keeping the room cool in summer and warm in the winter with less mechanical heating required.

Water will be collected from off the roofs and stored in a cistern that provides water for small pocket gardens around the home. Elsewhere, the natural grasses, which provide grazing for the couple's sheep, will be replanted to bring the indigenous landscape up to the edges of the house, creating a more seamless experience between land and home.

The ability for a residence in such an extreme climate to operate off the grid lies in the relationship of multiple strategies. An initial focus on passive conditions, construction materials and techniques, and the home's position in the landscape—a key factor in maximizing its energy efficiency—is critical. These considerations, along with highly efficient technologies employed for active energy requirements, such as a radiant-heat floor system, reduce the amount of energy required. There are several benefits to taking the time to consider what will be the interrelation between the different energy strategies you use. Here, one was a smaller financial investment in the photovoltaic and wind turbine technology. Another was the minimized impact on the landscape from the technologies themselves. In addition to the alternative energy system, a propane generator serves as backup and extra energy source should there be additional power requirements in severe winter conditions or a temporary loss of an energy source.

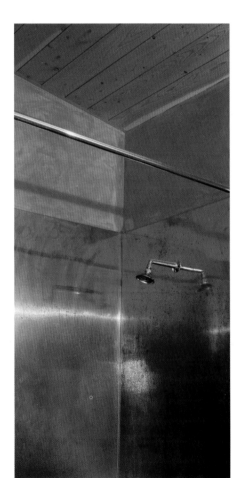

This page: The copper shower enclosure, which will age with use to a dark brown patina, complements the intense color of the bathroom's custom-tinted natural plaster walls polished with wax for water resistance.

Facing page: The living area has a shed roof pitched down to the north to minimize the exposure of the home to winter winds, helping to reduce heating requirements in the winter.

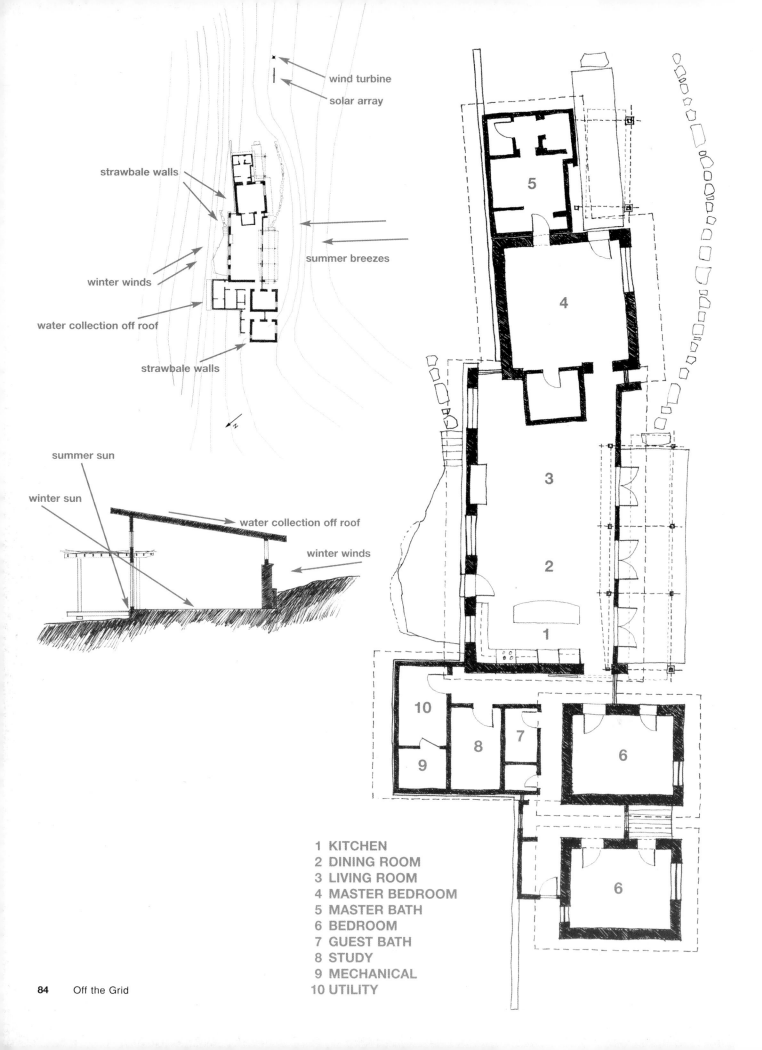

wind turbine

solar array

strawbale walls

summer breezes

winter winds

water collection off roof

strawbale walls

N

summer sun

winter sun

water collection off roof

winter winds

5

4

3

2

1

10

8

7

6

9

6

1 KITCHEN
2 DINING ROOM
3 LIVING ROOM
4 MASTER BEDROOM
5 MASTER BATH
6 BEDROOM
7 GUEST BATH
8 STUDY
9 MECHANICAL
10 UTILITY

View toward the master bedroom, along the southern wall. The pergola, which is also expressed on the outside deck, passes to the inside, creating a dynamic play of light on the floors.

Above: The wind turbine and photovoltaic hybrid system are situated away from the house to allow for maximum solar collection and ideal wind conditions. The freestanding forms have a sculptural quality against the open grassland.

Left: The study's strawbale wall holds a "truth window," enclosed simply in glass.

Simplified Living

Lake / Flato Architects   Hill Country Jacal   Pipe Creek, Texas

The Casey family retreat is located in the Texas Hill Country, forty miles outside of San Antonio. Named after the lean-to structures found in Mexico, the Jacal is a simple shelter designed with the thought that if left unattended it would disappear into the landscape in a hundred years.

The Texas Hill Country is a hot, humid environment, where built environments are typically air-conditioned for more than half of the year. Most people trade the actual experience of the place—the heat, sun, and humidity—for the ease of living in a controlled environment. Retreats are outfitted with a duplication of amenities found in primary residences, often with even larger garages to store additional cars and boats. The Caseys had different interests for their retreat. They envisioned a place that contrasted their day-to-day lives in a highly urban environment. They wanted a simple structure that would allow their family the opportunity to experience the "immediacy of a wilder landscape." Lake/Flato Architects interpreted the casualness of a jacal into a simple porch structure with a large shed roof for protection from the sun and a large stone wall for shelter from the north.

The Facts:

House: 925 square feet

Porch: 450 square feet

Technology
- A 5,000-gallon cistern holds water.
- A photovoltaic panel is used for heating water, and a six-panel system is for general use.
- A 12-battery storage system with inverter stores energy and acts as a backup.
- A Rumford fireplace, claimed to be one of the most efficient masonry fireplaces, heats the retreat.
- A composting toilet is used instead of a septic system.

Dynamic Use of Energy
- The photovoltaic panel provides energy for a water pump and additional electrical requirements.
- All general use of appliances, lighting, and basic electrical power is provided by the panels.
- Human energy is used to adjust the north-facing window "flaps" for ventilation as necessary.
- Compost from toilet can be used to enrich landscape soil.

Other Energy
- Propane supplies energy for a stove and refrigerator.

Materials of Interest
- Site-harvested cedar, a nonindigenous, invasive species, was used for posts and braces.
- Locally quarried limestone was used for building material.

This page: The deep porch, which shelters the space from sunlight in the summer, becomes a great sunporch in the winter. The deepness of the porch also allows the air to cool before reaching the center of the retreat.

Facing page: The experience of an exterior shower is revitalizing and invigorating. For a retreat it is a fantastic way to remind us that we are in a less controlled and contained environment. In many instances, when biodegradable soap is used, the water can be released directly back to the earth, a low-tech alternative to an unnecessary drain and septic system.

Above: At the retreat's eastern end, the stone wall houses the pump and mechanical system. The structure steps down from north to south, its southern edge a simple porch with a natural limestone patio and open views to the creek below.

Right: Detail of outdoor shower and toilet area at end of stone wall. The water, collected from the roof and stored in a cistern, is served by a pump employing energy created from a photovoltaic panel. The cedar limbs, collected on the site, help to shelter the shower from the blazing Texas heat. The toilet is a self-composting system that utilizes peat moss.

Fully independent from the grid, the Hill Country Jacal draws from the landscape and the cultural heritage of the area, both Hispanic and German, for its materials and construction methods. Set against the backdrop of indigenous live oaks and built from the local limestone, as were the homes of so many of the German settlers in the 1800s, the retreat rests on a stone escarpment that overlooks Bear Creek.

The large, highly insulated roof shelter provides cover from the sun for both screened and unscreened spaces. Housed within the stone wall are the kitchen, sleeping, and cooking alcoves along with a toilet and shower at one end and water pump at the other. The screened, open-space interior, oriented to let in prevailing summer winds, takes advantages of the breezes that are typical of the Hill Country. Ventilation flaps that allow the breeze to be controlled and the rising hot air to escape along the ceiling, are operated by a simple rope-and-pulley system located above the stone wall.

This page: With its fireplace at the center, the Hill Country Jacal is a dynamic demonstration of the open-living concept. Above the stone wall, operable ventilation "shutters" allow warm air to escape and draw cooler air in.

Facing page: The curved stone wall to the north, which blocks the winter wind, cups the space making the house feel more sheltered, while remaining open on three sides. Behind the wood ceiling, insulation has been added to protect the space from the hot Texas sun.

The Caseys consciously kept the home's energy requirements to a minimum in order to fulfill their goal of simplicity and minimal impact to the landscape; a propane tank provides energy for the stove and refrigerator. Rainwater is collected in a 5,000-gallon cistern and stored for bathing and cleaning. The shower, located beyond the screened room and exterior sink, allows for a more integrated experience in the landscape. The toilet, located with the shower, is self-composting and uses peat moss to aid the composting process. The cistern's pump and lighting are powered by a photovoltaic panel. Heat is provided by the Rumford fireplace, which is the centerpiece of the stone wall.

The Jacal's materials, including stone and cedar, were acquired locally, which not only creates the feeling that the shelter belongs to the place it is in, but is also a potent act of energy conservation and material sustainability.

The Jacal is an excellent example of how a simple retreat can offer rich experiences. Rather than duplicating the complications and infrastructure of a full-time home, this place offers solace and the opportunity to be closer to the land on which we live.

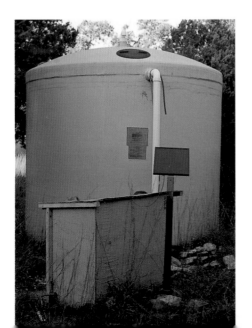

Above: The retreat honors the cultural heritage of the region through a contemporary retelling of the *jacal,* a Hispanic term for a "lean-to." The shed roof resting upon the curved limestone wall plays out this concept beautifully.

Left: A 5,000-gallon, fiberglass cistern stores rainwater collected from the roof, enough for all the retreat's needs. A small photovoltaic panel generates energy to pump water to the pump room, located at the end of the stone wall, adjacent to the kitchen. With the pump in line, conventional plumbing pipe may be used to move water to the kitchen and shower.

Facing page: Designed for effective passive solar heating, the winter sun reaches far into the screened retreat, but blocks sun in the summer as the solar angle changes.

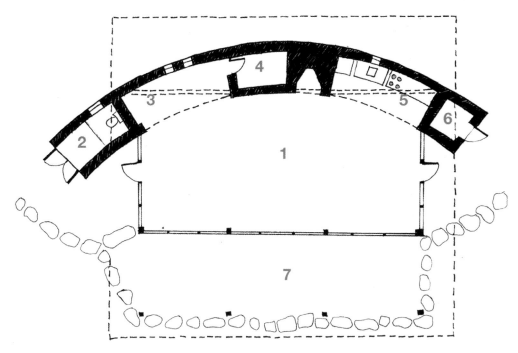

1 COMMON LIVING AREA
2 BATHROOM
3 SLEEPING
4 STORAGE
5 KITCHEN
6 WATER COLLECTION
7 COVERED PORCH

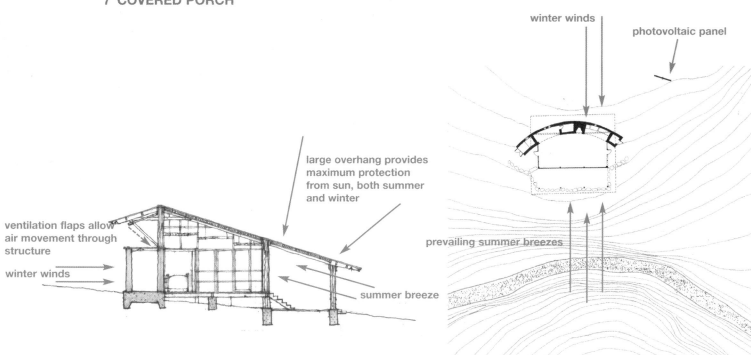

ventilation flaps allow air movement through structure

winter winds

large overhang provides maximum protection from sun, both summer and winter

summer breeze

winter winds

photovoltaic panel

prevailing summer breezes

Operable "shutters" are hinged with a pulley system that allows them to be opened and shut for ventilation without climbing a ladder.

Suburban Footprint

Arkin/Tilt Architects   D'Souza and de la Torre Residence   Belmont, California

The D'Souza and de la Torre residence is situated on a corner parcel in the dense suburban community that extends from San Francisco into the surrounding hills and coastal peninsula. With a setting of mature, coastal oak trees, one of the initial goals of the clients and architect, in addition to creating a sustainable home, was to retain the beauty of the trees. Through a variance, the siting of the home was moved closer to the street to protect the trees. The result is a home that presents a townhouse sensibility to the street, softened by an entry terrace court that creates a comfortable relationship between domestic space and community.

The Facts:

Home: 1,823 square feet

Technology
- 20 150-watt photovoltaic panels from BP
- Sunny Boy inverter from SMA America
- Gobi solar water heater from Heliodyne

Dynamic Use of Energy
- A solar water heater generates heat for radiant floors and domestic hot water.
- The photovoltaic panel doubles as a power generator and a sun-shielding awning.

Other Energy
- The municipal system provides additional electricity.
- The municipal system provides water.
- A gas-fired boiler provides backup heat.

Materials of Interest
- Reclaimed Douglas fir for wall and bookshelf framing
- Trusses of salvaged beams
- Ceiling decking of vinegar barrel staves
- Exterior soffit of salvaged siding
- Salvaged doors
- Sliding doors and screen panels of sustainably harvested Spanish cedar
- Roof shingles of recycled automobile tires
- Recycled-glass countertops

This page: The primary living space is open from kitchen to dining room and living room. The structural trusses are built from salvaged beams. The concrete floor, which acts as a passive solar heat sink and shelters a deep sand bed for the collection and storage of heat, is stained to complement the color palette of the natural materials.

Facing page: Photovoltaic panels serve as an awning in the home's entry court and an announcement to a busy public street of the owners' commitment to the environment.

D'Souza and de la Torre came to David Arkin of Arkin/Tilt Architects with a rich list of goals for their home's character and engagement in issues of sustainability. A key guide for the formal characteristic of the home is the cultural heritage of the clients—urban Mexico and India—whose architectural heritages include private courtyards, towers, and thick walls. The result is a home that honors these qualities while fitting within the context of the community in which it is situated. Entry into the home is casual: through the entry court or from the garage, which is tied to the home through a stairway core. The home's 1,823 square feet are layered with multiple functions, providing a rich and comfortable experience for the residents while retaining a small footprint. The stair core blends into a multilevel library and also shares its openness with the light and ventilation tower above, creating an inviting series of interior terraces that double as an integrated system for passive ventilation throughout the home. The photovoltaic panels and solar hot-water system are integrated within the roof and awning system, while a roof trellis protects the roof terrace from summer sun. The home's southeast orientation allows morning sun into the kitchen and living spaces on the main floor and the proper orientation for the solar collection panels on the roof.

Above: Arriving from the garage, one enters into a well-lit public space.

Left: The home's design takes advantage of the steeply sloping site by tucking the garage under the home, along a side street. This strategy also decreases the impact the garage has on the overall experience of the house, retaining a public entry court on the primary street front.

Right: View from street with visible roof-mounted photovoltaic panel. The stair tower terminates at a door to the roof balcony.

The home operates as a grid intertie, with the photovoltaic and solar hot-water panels actively reducing energy reliance on the municipal infrastructure. Because the home is located in a moderate climate, the solar hot-water panels can be used to generate the heat for the radiant floor system that runs through a deep sand bed below the home's concrete slab. This highly efficient system heats the mass of the sand and concrete, allowing the heat to be stored for a long period of time and then released slowly through the floor slab. In the summer, this system also provides domestic hot water, which is stored in a tank. Primary hot water comes from a conventional hot-water system. A "shunt loop" is incorporated into the solar hot-water system so that in the summer additional heat collected from the system can run through exterior patio slabs, warming the outside spaces and extending use of the patios into the cool, humid nights prevalent along the California coast.

Other passive and energy-efficient strategies incorporated into the home include exterior walls with a double-insulation system where sprayed cellulose fills the wall cavities and is combined with rigid board beyond the exterior sheathing. Thermal mass is provided in the living and dining rooms: concrete-block walls with filled cavities are finished with a stucco/plaster surface. The sun heats up the walls by day through the south-facing windows. As the evening chill sets in, they release their stored heat into the living and dining room area.

This page: The laundry area is tucked away from the open living area, but remains in proximity to the activity of the kitchen. Highly energy-efficient appliances are employed to reduce the overall energy load created by the house and reduce the amount of water used in washing.

Facing page, above: The guest bedroom, though small in scale, is a well-thought-out design that includes beds on casters with storage drawers below to reduce the need for freestanding dressers.

Facing page, below: The extra-large stair landing becomes a space for the library and study supported by the dynamic use of natural light, which filters through the stair tower.

Above and below: A wall of books at the stair landing provides an excellent location for a library, a place that calls us to pause and contemplate before moving on.

Facing page: View from dining area through kitchen and into stair tower beyond, allows for "night flushing" through the stair tower windows. The well-planned placement of glass diminishes the need for general lighting throughout the house, and reduces the overall energy load created by the house.

Because the grid intertie is so reliable, no battery backup system is employed, although a gas-fired backup system is set up to provide additional energy for unusually cold periods. The photovoltaic system's 3-kilowatt array is sized to produce approximately half of the energy required for a typical home in California over the period of a year. But as this home has been designed to operate as efficiently as possible, with additional insulation and a passive-solar-and-ventilation strategy, it takes much less overall energy than is typically required to provide a thermally comfortable home in California. D'Souza and de la Torre's objective is to engage the home's passive strategies as much as possible in order to reduce its overall energy consumption, while practicing a more sustainable lifestyle.

1 ENTRY TERRACE
2 LIVING ROOM
3 DINING ROOM
4 KITCHEN
5 BATH
6 PANTRY
7 GUEST BEDROOM
8 PLAY/STUDY
9 BATH
10 BEDROOM
11 LIBRARY
12 BATH
13 MASTER BEDROOM
14 ROOF TERRACE
15 TOWER

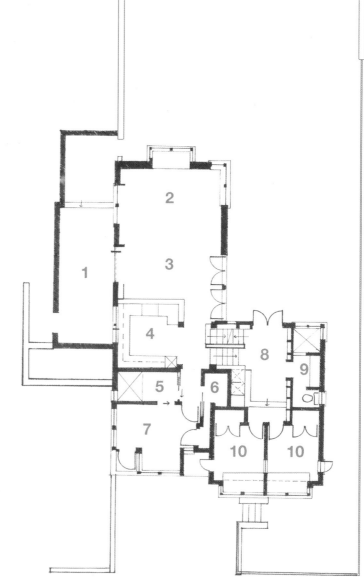

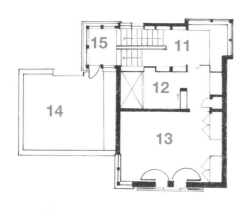

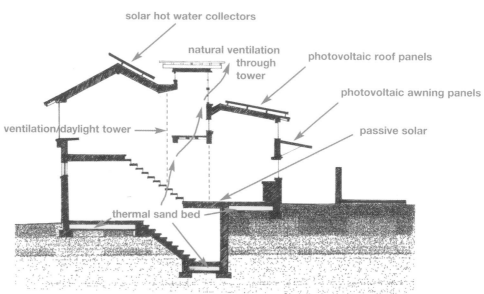

solar hot water collectors

natural ventilation through tower

photovoltaic roof panels

photovoltaic awning panels

ventilation/daylight tower

passive solar

thermal sand bed

Large windows provide plenty of natural lighting in the stair landing's office/study space.

Above: From counter to backsplash to bar counter, kitchen surface transitions are a harmonious collection of recycled glass.

Left: From the kitchen, the stair to upper bedrooms and the garage entry become a pivotal point in the house for circulation, airflow, and daylighting.

Right: The mechanical room includes boilers for radiant heat and a system for net metering photovoltaic-derived energy.

Metropolitan Redo

John Petrarca, Architect   Reade Street Townhouse   New York City, New York

New York City is a place full of inspiration and challenges. The city is constantly evolving as small neighborhoods are redeveloped from industrial warehouses or small tenement houses to well-appointed homes for those who are fortunate enough to afford them. John Petrarca and his wife Sarah Bartlett share a parallel story of inspiration and challenge in the townhouses they built in the now-gentrified and popular Tribeca area of lower Manhattan. On micro and macro levels, this area is a successfully sustainable environment due to the contributions of people like Petrarca. Petrarca's professional commitment to more energy-conscious design led him to propose a series of townhouses that would be served by the geothermal qualities that lie below the granite rock on which Manhattan rests.

While not fully independent from the grid, the townhouses are a testament to what is possible with vision and tenacity. After purchasing several adjacent and surrounding buildings in his neighborhood, John Petrarca took on the task of redeveloping the land into a well-designed group of townhouses. His vision was quite unique; he was interested in building with energy-resourceful materials and relying on a natural condition of the earth to heat, cool, and provide hot water for the townhouses.

The Facts:

Home: 6,500 square feet (including leased office space on the first floor and cellar)

Technology
- The geothermal exchange was rated by the EPA as one of the lowest-life-cycle-cost systems available, and also one of the lowest-emission-producing systems.

Dynamic Use of Energy
- Geothermal energy provides for all hot water requirements as well as heating and cooling throughout the year.
- The heating system works through a highly efficient radiant-heat floor system.

Other Energy
- Grid-tied electricity
- Grid-tied gas
- Grid-tied water supply and septic systems

Materials of Interest
- Insulated Concrete Forms (ICF), a highly efficient, insulated-wall material, are used for primary construction walls.
- Low-VOC (volatile organic compound) paints are used throughout.
- Kitchen cabinets are covered in Marmoleum, a natural product made from linseed oil, wood flour, pine rosin, and jute.

This page: The townhouse glows at night, reflecting its light to the street below. Here it can be seen in scale with its neighbors, its pioneering use of geothermal energy to heat and cool it quietly conserving limited natural resources.

Facing page: The view from dining room into kitchen shares light and views to the south and street, which brings in sunlight for passive solar heating. Limestone floors provide some heat sink properties as they retain solar heat gained throughout the day.

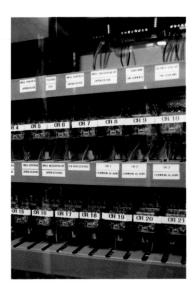

The concept is simple. Below the earth's immediate surface its temperature stabilizes, remaining at an almost-constant 52 degrees. Tapping into this constant temperature for heating and cooling requirements can greatly reduce a building's required overall energy loads. Petrarca took this concept and tied it with a heat-pump source. In the summer, the heat pump uses the energy from excess heat above ground to bring cool, belowground air to the surface. In the winter, a similar process is employed: the air from below ground, which is already much warmer than the outside air, is brought into the heating system and minimal energy is needed to heat the air to its final temperature.

Petrarca pursued his vision of more resourceful urban living. Along the way, he gained the attention of the EPA, who supported his plan by helping institute ways to apply alternative energy in a city already stressed with its large conventional-energy requirements.

Facing page: The south-facing deck off the penthouse, a dream for most urban dwellers.

This page, above: The control panel and circuitry required for the geothermal heating and cooling system. The system uses belowground air or water, which maintains a constant 56 degrees, and a heat exchanger to boost the desired temperature up or down with less overall generated-energy required. The efficiency of this system has made it popular across the nation as people search for more efficient ways to maintain their homes.

This page, left: The study, with highly desirable southern light not often acquired in New York City. An open, interior balcony to below increases the expansive experience of the space and connects the living spaces of the home vertically.

Petrarca's townhouse, along with the others, benefits from the system in a number of ways. The home is heated with a radiant-heat floor system, one of the most comfortable heating systems available. In addition, the system provides all of the hot water required for the home. Only a small amount of electricity is required to run the pump itself.

The perimeter walls are built from Insulated Concrete Forms (ICFs), which provide a high degree of insulation when the forms are filled with concrete. The building's façade was inspired by the surrounding buildings' circa-1800s cast-iron façades. Built of steel and fabricated off-site in a local bridge shop, the façade was assembled street-side and put in place in a manner similar to old-fashioned barn raisings, with the steel welders assembling the structure on-site. The steel system allowed for large window openings that blended the new building with its surroundings and allowed for large amounts of natural light to filter through the home.

This page, top: The mechanical room, which houses the components for the geothermal system employed for both the radiant-heat system in the floors for winter and the forced-air system for cool air in the summer. The system is a very effective alternative energy system for a highly urban area where sunlight and wind are too often affected by high-rise neighbors and building orientation.

This page, above: Clearly labeled piping in the mechanical room makes any subsequent maintenance less troublesome and allows the owners to use the system to educate visitors about the geothermal operation.

Facing page: The living room has a lowered wood ceiling, an exception to the painted walls, that increases the intimacy and particularity of the space. A real wood-burning fireplace set within a tile-stone wall is reminiscent of the large fireplace "rooms" found in houses of the early 1900s.

The narrow lot (25 feet wide and 54 feet deep) resulted in a home that is vertically stacked, rather than spread out horizontally. Discrete parts of the home are discovered through a stair that winds along one side of the building. An open-plan kitchen and living area with large south-facing windows occupy the fourth and fifth floors. The second floor houses the children's bedrooms, bathrooms, and playroom; the master bedroom suite is located on the third floor. A rooftop penthouse provides a guest suite and terrace with views to the south. The feeling of the home is both urban and natural with simple, clean details and a palette of materials that include limestone, rough-cut marble, steel, and wood.

The Reade Street Townhouse, completed in 2001, also serves as John Petrarca's professional legacy since his passing in 2003. The project is not only a dynamic system of energy conservation but also provides a positive vision for urban living with great aspirations for life and community.

Left: The kitchen, with cabinetry by Bulthaup, is detailed with stainless steel. The island, while remaining open through the space, helps to define the kitchen and dining area.

Below: The dining room, looking down from the balcony of the study above.

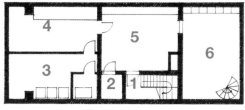

Basement

Fourth Floor

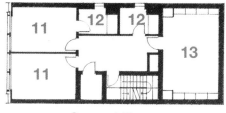

First Floor

Fifth Floor

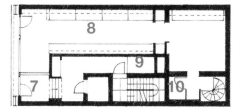

Second Floor

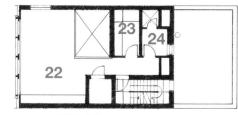

Sixth Floor

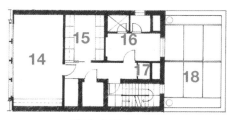

Third Floor

Balcony

1 STAIR
2 ELEVATOR
3 MECHANICAL
4 WORKSHOP
5 STORAGE
6 CONFERENCE ROOM
7 RESIDENTIAL ENTRY
8 HOME OFFICE
9 TRASH
10 BATHROOM
11 KID'S BEDROOM
12 BATHROOM
13 PLAYROOM
14 MASTER BEDROOM
15 DRESSING
16 MASTER BATH
17 ELECTRONICS
18 SKYLIGHT
19 KITCHEN
20 DINING
21 LIVING
22 STUDY
23 PANTRY LAUNDRY
24 GUEST BATHROOM
25 TERRACE
26 PENTHOUSE GUEST
27 CANOPY
28 UPPER ROOF TERRACE
29 SKYLIGHT

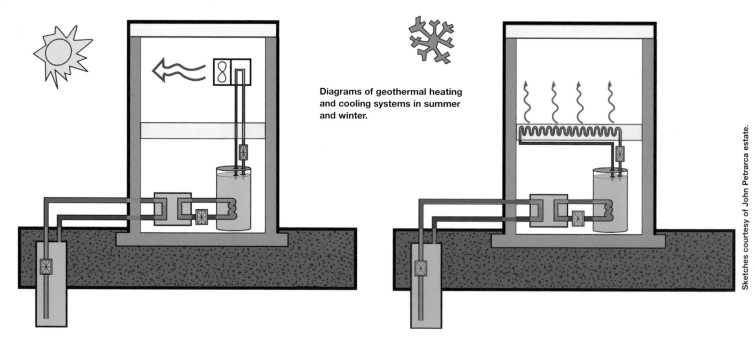

Diagrams of geothermal heating and cooling systems in summer and winter.

This page: Master bathroom with limestone-tile walls, third floor. The neutral color and material palette of this room, along with its natural details, help to make it a true refuge in a city that is constantly evolving and often challenging.

Facing page, left: This diagram refers to the system's draw from ground air to reduce the energy required to fully cool a home in the summer time through a forced-air system.

Facing page, right: This diagram refers to the system's draw from the ground air to reduce the energy required to fully heat a home through its radiant-heat floor system.

Above: The stairwell through the townhouse serves as the vertical entry sequence. Its vibrant red color emphasizes the continuity of the volume with a recycled-glass and steel stair sliding up through the space. A sheet of woven stainless-steel mesh serves as the inside barrier in lieu of a handrail.

Right: The fourth floor of the living space, which includes the living room, kitchen, and dining area, connects to the double-height study space above.

Facing page: Mosaic tiles provide a great play of light and visual interest in a small space.

House R128 challenges our assumptions of the technological potential of homes. Designed from the point of view that architecture should contribute to the cultural spirit of the twenty-first century but also be responsive to the current stresses on the natural environment, the home is designed to be fully emission free and as energy conscious as possible. House R128 also serves as a challenge to fellow practitioners for, as Werner Sobek says, "Building construction evinces none of the innovative dynamics found, for instance, in the automobile industry, where the latest developments in computers, materials, and sensor technology are combined to produce unique synergetic effects."

The pioneering attitude that Sobek applied throughout House R128 is infused with a contemporary understanding of home and architecture, from the basic system of construction to the finish details to the technologies employed in the grid-intertied home. At the same time, the inspiration for the home is drawn from a traditional tower home found in North Yemen, a place the architect and his wife have spent some time. At the top of these homes is found a *mafraj*, the "room in which the important things in life are discussed." Ursula Sobek adds, "The feeling of absolute freedom and intimate contact with nature was overwhelming. The desire to live as in a *mafraj* remained with us after this experience."

The Facts:

House: 2,706 square feet

Technology
- Geothermal energy powers a heat exchanger and cross-flow heat exchanger.
- Triple-glazed, glass-curtain wall system with reflective plastic foil inserts and inert gas reduces heat gain in house.
- 48 frameless photovoltaic panels are located on the roof with an ideal output of 6.72 kilowatts per hour.

Dynamic Use of Energy
- Earth-moderated air is brought into the exchange air system and heated or cooled as required.
- Photovoltaic panels generate energy for the heat exchange system.

Other Energy
- Electrical requirements, water, and sewage are grid-intertied.

Materials of Interest
- Primary structure is a bolted, recyclable steel frame based on a twelve-point grid system. The entire system weighs only 87,744 pounds.
- Triple-glazed, glass window units are from Glas-Fischer, Murr.

This page: House R128 fully lit at night glows like an x-ray, showing all the parts as a whole for the viewer's benefit. Imagine the house, instead, as it must be on most nights, with task lights floating in the darkness of the surrounding landscape.

Facing page: The transparency of the stair allows the house, a creation of cutting-edge technology expressed through a poetic translation, to be experienced as a whole.

This page: The balcony projecting from the house also functions as a bridge back to the hillside.

Facing page: The kitchen, built only of lower cabinets, provides uninterrupted views across the house from one window wall to the other.

The home is designed to be totally recyclable, from modular component parts to lightweight materials. The heating and air-conditioning system draws its primary energy requirements from roof-mounted photovoltaic panels and a sophisticated geothermal system. The house's glass and load-bearing steel frame permits full visual access to the surrounding landscape and views of Stuttgart. Entry to the home is along a passage through the woods. A continuous stair takes one up four floors and into the dining, kitchen, and living levels, reminiscent of the *mafraj*. Although a discreet, two-story enclosed space holds the more private necessities of the bathrooms, all other living activities are experienced in the open space of the home.

The geothermal-activated heating and cooling system runs through metal panels in the ceilings, maintaining a constant temperature with coils that carry cool or warm water as appropriate for the season. Fresh air is exchanged through an underground channel loop that brings the incoming air to a warmer temperature in the winter and a cooler temperature in the summer. Allowing the thermal capacity of the earth to moderate the outside air prior to bringing it into the home greatly reduces the energy required for the system. In the winter, as the heated internal air is exchanged for fresh air, a cross-flow heat exchanger is used to "pre-heat" the incoming air, thus reducing the amount of energy required to bring the incoming air up to the desired temperature. In the summer the same system is employed to cool the incoming air, with zero energy required. While heat radiates from the ceiling panels in the winter, in the summer, heat is absorbed into the ceiling system, transferred through a heat exchanger and retained in a long-term storage system, then returned in the winter as heat during the vacillations of temperature over the day and night. It is a simple internal cycle of exchange from cool to warm water throughout the year, which adds to the efficiency of the geothermal aspects. The photovoltaic panels, located on the roof, provide the energy required for the ventilation system and the heat pump. Overall, the panels help reduce grid energy use in a system that is already highly efficient.

House R128 extends the use of technological innovations into sensors employed throughout. As Werner Sobek points out, sensor technology was not used as an end in itself, just where it made life easier. Temperature and lighting levels can be controlled with touch screens; lighting and doors can be controlled by voice. Water flow and temperature are also controlled with sensor technology. A core of cables and plumbing pipes are visible design components of the home and will permit easy technological updating of the systems in the years to come. The system of construction, structure, and technology are integral to the design, rather than functional aspects to be covered over with additional material. This philosophy results in less material used in the house.

Large triple-glazed glass with a metal-coated plastic foil, and inert gas between panes, reduces the long-wave sun rays, thereby reducing heat gain in the home. Remote-operated windows on every floor allow for ventilation throughout the house.

Above: The bathroom volumes, stacked vertically one over the other for efficiency of technological installation and hot air exchange throughout the house, are the home's only enclosed spaces.

Right: Large operable windows, with views out to the city below, allow for fresh air exchange.

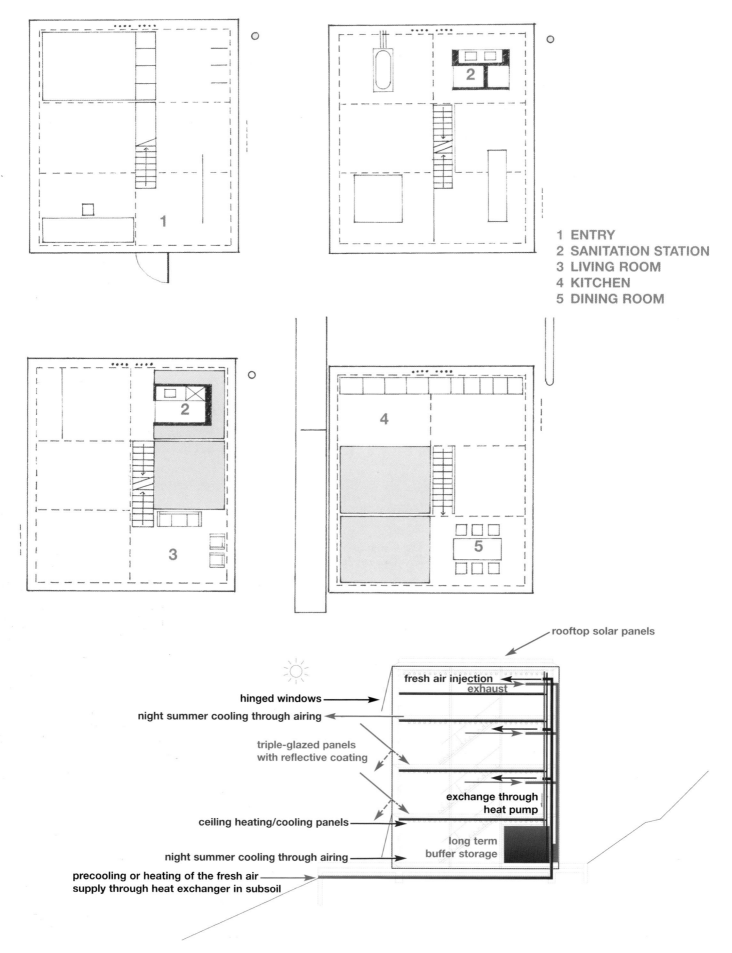

1 ENTRY
2 SANITATION STATION
3 LIVING ROOM
4 KITCHEN
5 DINING ROOM

rooftop solar panels

fresh air injection
exhaust

hinged windows

night summer cooling through airing

triple-glazed panels
with reflective coating

exchange through
heat pump

ceiling heating/cooling panels

night summer cooling through airing

long term
buffer storage

precooling or heating of the fresh air
supply through heat exchanger in subsoil

Prefabricated wood panels were placed between the floor beams without fasteners, an efficient system that uses less materials. The aluminum ceiling panels are clipped to the ceiling, providing acoustic benefits as well as the means for the heating and cooling system. Minimal furniture is used throughout the house, with several pieces designed by the architect to work seamlessly with the home and reduce clutter. The bathtub is freestanding and can be connected anywhere in the house that provides a plumbing connection through a flexible connector system.

House R128 is an unusual vision for a home to most eyes. Ursula Sobek makes our understanding of the home's potential clear with her beautifully stated personal experience. "At the breakfast table on the top floor," she writes, "I can let my eyes roam across the city of Stuttgart and quietly pursue my dreams. This gives me the feeling of being free, which is important to me. Here I can breathe freely. Sometimes it is difficult to get up from the breakfast table and get to grips with the day, one simply wants to sit there forever. This same experience is shared by our guests who come for dinner and look down on the nocturnal sea of lights. Not infrequently, dawn is rising when they wend their way home."

Photovoltaic panels mounted on the roof are an integral part of the home's design, and an integral part of the home's off-the-grid energy system. A large conduit running parallel to the entry bridge provides a connection to the surrounding infrastructure brought in through the lower level.

Above: The metal panels in the ceiling enclose the tubes that are filled with water. The water is moderated between hot and cold to heat or cool the house with the geothermal technology and combined heat exchanger. The heating/cooling panels occupy about 40 percent of the ceiling, allowing for a low degree of temperature exchange, resulting in an even temperature throughout.

Right: The reflectivity of the glass captures the building's surroundings in its façade, blending the house with the landscape.

Sustainability on a Budget

Breathe Architects   Wilson Residence   Mono Mills, Ontario

John Wilson and his partner, Leigh Geraghty, are thoroughly committed to conserving resources and reducing their energy consumption. As John Wilson states in his manifesto *Natural Living*, his life changed with the birth of his first child. "At that moment I literally felt my connection with the infinite, to nature and to time." Wilson felt that he needed to create a "lifestyle that would nurture [his] children's creative potential while providing a model for living that, if adopted by a large enough portion of the world's population, would ensure a safe, healthy, and sustainable world for the future."

The Facts:

Home: 2,500 square feet

Technology
- Solar energy is collected in 10 Shell ST-40 thin-film solar modules.
- A Bergey XL 1 wind turbine collects wind energy.
- Collected energy is run through a Xantrex PS 2500 inverter and stored in a minimal battery bank.
- Rainwater is collected for most, and eventually will be used for all, domestic water uses.
- A "living machine" system will be installed in the future for waste management.

Dynamic Use of Energy
- Passive solar heat is gathered in the concrete floor, which is also heated by a radiant system as necessary.
- A photovoltaic array and wind turbine are complementary, potential energy creators in summer and winter for all electrical requirements.
- Greenhouse-generated passive heat aids to warm the home.

Other Energy
- An EPA-rated woodstove from Pacific Energy helps heat the home.
- The municipal energy system provides all other necessary energy.
- A well provides necessary domestic water until rainwater and gray-water systems are in use.

Materials of Interest
- Sod roof for highly insulated roofing
- Strawbale walls
- Bamboo flooring

This page: Wilson's wind turbine, seen through the living room window, is an unobtrusive part of the landscape. Wind turbines generate energy with a minimum speed of 8 mph.

Facing page: The house is oriented to the south for passive solar intake through large windows. Photovoltaic panels are mounted above the windows, blending with the metal which wraps down from the roof.

This page, above: The concrete floor in this greenhouse gallery passively absorbs, retains, and releases the sun that comes in through all the windows.

This page, below: The gallery hall with strawbale wall exterior. Pebbles at floor act as a "vent cover" for cool air to vent up from the basement and through the house, exiting through the open skylight. The pebbles also serve as an inventive transition between the irregular strawbale wall and the uniformity of the tile floor. A strawbale "truth window" greets visitors in the entry hall.

Facing page: The beauty of the stucco strawbale wall is warmed by the bamboo floor. The simple materials of this home provide an elegance that is honest in their expression. The mirror above the sideboard borrows light from the windows on the opposite wall creating dynamic movement in the space.

One of the results of this lifestyle commitment is the home at Mono Mills. For Wilson and Geraghty the home is an organic process; their lifestyle goals will continue to evolve and impact the home and surrounding landscape over the next several years. For the architect, Martin Liefhebber, the home offered the opportunity to work with clients who were fully committed and passionate about achieving a great design that was as sustainable as possible given their budget. The project also serves as an example of interests that are challenged by the conventions of municipalities. Wilson's goal to rely less on the grid and conventional modes of waste and water management were at odds with the legal requirements of his community. In the end, as many people discover, building decisions must balance best-case scenarios for the environment and resource conservation and reasonable budget constraints. For example, Wilson's goal of installing composting toilets was squelched after the city required the installation of a conventional septic system with drain field for at least one toilet. The cost of the conventional system took the money needed for the composting toilets, leaving Wilson with no immediate options but to use the septic system and wait to install a composting toilet as finances allowed. What will be the finished result of Wilson's experiment in living is somewhere in the future. The family's personal goals for a healthier environment will be reached at a double-the-money investment after the expectations of the municipality are achieved. But despite the government roadblocks, the Wilson residence offers much to consider and appreciate.

Designed with a grid-intertied system of photovoltaic panels and a small wind turbine, the home generates approximately 50 percent of its energy requirements for heating, appliances, and other electrical needs. The photovoltaic array is mounted on the south-facing dormer roof with a tracking system to optimize the solar collection, while the wind turbine is located away from the home, sited for optimal wind collection.

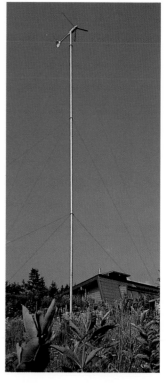

This page: The wood-burning stove, centered in the house, provides efficient use of its heat through the chimney pipe that extends through the double-height space.

Facing page, above: Entry to the house is flanked by the carport and topped with a roof the owners intend to plant for a future "green roof."

Facing page, below: Wind turbine with house beyond. Wind turbines need to be clear from obstructions and are typically installed for residences sited on an acre or more of land. Most domestic-scale turbines are 80–120 feet tall, with blades extending 21 feet in diameter.

Two significant formal aspects shape the experience of the home. First is a large, shedlike green roof that extends over the carport and home. This structure both blends the home into the landscape and provides significant insulation. The second is a passive ventilation system located at the center and top of the home that brings in indirect light from the south and allows the house to exchange warm air for cool in a continuous loop when the lower windows are open. A strawbale wall to the north provides superior insulation from the north winds in the winter, while a modified post-and-beam system carries the structural loads and a wood-frame wall to the south, allowing large window openings for passive solar heat collection in the concrete floor slab. A central wood-burning stove augments the radiant-heat floors during Ontario's harsh winter months. The tiered floor plan, with primary living spaces on the ground floor and bedrooms above, is an open design with circulation through the center to encourage the movement of air, heat, and sunlight throughout the home. Water is collected from the roof and stored in a cistern. In the future, a filter system will be installed to provide clean drinking water from the cistern. A long-time dream of Wilson's was realized in a greenhouse being built along the home's south side. A densely planted greenhouse next to a wall can modify a home's interior environment as plants create their own microclimate, reducing the overall need for a system to heat or cool the home. In addition, the greenhouse will extend the growing season of edible plants into winter and humidify the air.

This page: View of the kitchen and living room with second floor above supported by a structure of parallams, an engineered wood product manufactured from fast-growing trees, that provides superior rigidity and strength for supporting the roof.

Facing page: The Wilson home at twilight.

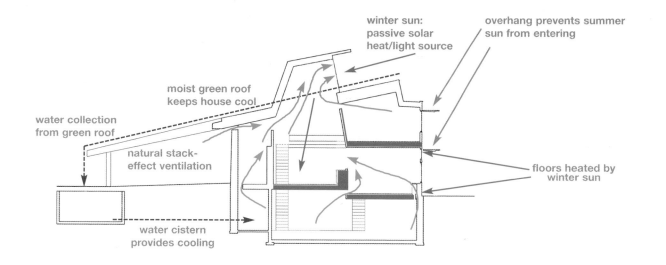

winter sun:
passive solar
heat/light source

overhang prevents summer
sun from entering

moist green roof
keeps house cool

water collection
from green roof

natural stack-
effect ventilation

floors heated by
winter sun

water cistern
provides cooling

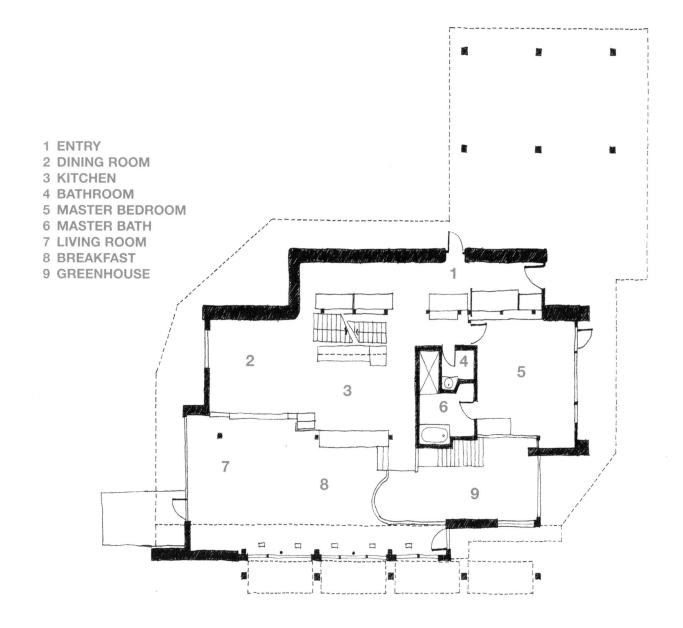

1 ENTRY
2 DINING ROOM
3 KITCHEN
4 BATHROOM
5 MASTER BEDROOM
6 MASTER BATH
7 LIVING ROOM
8 BREAKFAST
9 GREENHOUSE

Simple materials are used throughout this home, including the plywood floors at the second-floor balcony, which are finished with a clear seal. The double-height space combined with the open balcony allows the heat from the stove to warm the entire house.

Four Horizons is located along the eastern coast of Australia, on the crest of a ridge at the northern edge of Watagans National Park, looking out onto the lower Hunt Valley. The locale is a truly remote environment where municipal systems of any type are unavailable. For Lindsay Johnston, the Autonomous House grew out of a personal challenge of self-sufficiency along with a commitment to take responsibility for how resources are used. In 1993, Johnston, an architect and professor, moved his home base from the city to Watagans National Park. Knowing that external opportunities for water, plumbing, power and communications were nonexistent, Johnston took on the serious task of designing the most efficient, well-designed, least environmentally obtrusive compound that could be built.

The Facts:

House: 1,800 square feet

Breezeway: 820 square feet

Technology

- Wood-burning stove and fireplace
- 8 55-watt photovoltaic panels by BP, plus solar power for telecommunication
- A battery bank of 24 BP no. 2P566 batteries
- Solar water heaters
- Water collection cisterns
- Dual-flush toilet

Dynamic Use of Energy

- A solar-powered uplink powers telecommunications.
- A wood-burning stove provides heat for the house; all the wood is collected from the forest floor, reducing the risk of fast-moving brush fires in the area.
- The town sports car was traded in for a more efficient 650cc 2-cylinder Subaru.
- Gray water from domestic use is used to water the vegetable garden.
- Water collection, in three locations, is used for domestic requirements, the vegetable garden, and fire-suppression support.
- Solar water heaters heat all domestic hot water.
- The dual-flush toilet conserves clean water, using it first in the sink and then for flushing.

Other Energy

- Food refrigeration and cooking, and hot water backup are powered by propane.
- A generator by Lister is used for backup electrical requirements and powered by diesel.
- A conventional septic system was installed for toilet discharge only.

Materials of Interest

- Recycled poly/wool wall insulation
- "Color panel" steel agricultural frames made in Australia
- Concrete floors finished with Livos Hard Oil and Livos Glevivo Liquid Wax, products that contain beeswax, shellac wax, pine oil, rosemary oil, and carnuba wax

This page: The end of the living volume opening onto the courtyard breezeway makes visible the double-roofed system and its rooftop ventilation for the escape of hot air. The cap is made from a transparent material doubling as a skylight.

Facing page: Winter sun stretches across the landscape, moving into the house. Concrete floors act as a heat sink to retain the solar heat throughout the night.

Autonomous House is a study in observation, measure, and care. Two separate interior spaces, which contain the basics of the two-bedroom house, are joined together by an outdoor room with a preexisting fireplace, to create a center for the new home. The living spaces are sheltered by an independent roof that floats over the enclosures, providing additional insulation and protection. The "fly" roof was developed from the agricultural steel shed frame, locally manufactured in New South Wales, and a common sight in this rural, agricultural area. The environmental lessons of Autonomous House do not stop at its doorway. Vegetable garden, solar panels, water collection, and the volume of gas that would be used in the car to get to and from the home were all considered when Johnston was determining the viability and credibility of living off the grid. Electricity, provided by a 440-watt array and a battery bank that stores power generated from the array, is incorporated as is a diesel generator. All water for the house is collected from the roofs of the house and garage and stored in steel and concrete tanks. The full tanks provide six months of water use. Located in the tree-shaded western side of the house and throughout the compound, they store an excess of water, ensuring a supply in case of drought or fire. Additional water is collected off of the stable roof for the garden and a dedicated firefighting supply.

This page: The courtyard breezeway, opening out to the valley view, is held between the two interior volumes, offering an exterior fireplace, hinged panels for reducing winter winds, and the opportunity to extend living to the outside while remaining covered. The roof superstructure provides a temperate canopy from inclement weather.

Facing page: Water-collection cisterns hold enough rainwater for all required water throughout the year: domestic water use, watering the gardens, and a six-month supply of water in case of drought or fire.

The inner workings of the home are well thought out and regularly monitored. The energy required for the refrigerator and stove is supplied by propane gas. Water is entirely heated by a rooftop, solar hot-water panel in the summer, with winter hot water backup provided by an integral propane backup boiler on the roof (the house requires an average of 18.7 pounds of propane fuel per week). Both of the interior spaces have wood-burning stoves to provide heat in the winter. The stove, located in the public side of the house, also serves as a baker's oven and cooktop. A dual-flush toilet, where water is first used for washing hands, then held for flushing, helps conserve water, releasing its discharge into a conventional septic system and drain field. All gray water from showers, sinks, and laundry is used to irrigate the garden.

Above: The "aperture" window in the bathroom shares the view to the outside through the bedroom, a great strategy for compact living.

Left: The living area presents a design strategy employed throughout both living volumes: minimal walls held down from the ceiling provide for great ventilation across the house.

In order to develop an energy-efficient building, specific materials of construction and passive energy strategies were incorporated. The home is oriented to allow winter sun to enter the living areas, while the "fly"-roof overhang blocks out the high summer sun. In the summer, the center court collects breezes coming from the ocean, cooling the shaded interior and exterior rooms. The exterior room can also be shut off from these breezes in the winter. Large north-facing windows collect winter sun and small south-facing windows minimize the effect of winter weather. A filled-concrete-block wall runs through the middle of the interior portions of the house, providing a thermal mass that stores winter sun for release into the rooms later in the day. Concrete floors and exterior block walls provide thermal mass to retain coolness in the summer and warmth in the winter. The exterior of the building's south, east, and west exterior walls are clad with small-profile corrugated steel and insulated with recycled polyester/wool insulation.

The Autonomous House demonstrates that living can occur quite conscientiously even when some energy needs require fossil fuel. Overall, the embodied energy and energy consumption of this house is less than that of a typical grid-intertied home. Future improvements could be made with additional photovoltaic panels and/or a wind turbine to make the home even more self-sufficient and less reliant on the limited resources of the planet.

Above: A small solar-powered satellite tower provides the connection for phone and Internet.

Left: The bedroom's lowered interior wall allows cross ventilation, an effective passive cooling strategy.

Right: Detail of hinged, metal door shutters, which provide versatility to the glass-door openings. The doors operate independently allowing for passage or blockage of light, depending on the season. They can also close completely in harsh weather or when the family is away. The roof super-structure, which encompasses the entire interior space, has a large rain gutter attached to capture all water and collect it into the cisterns throughout the home.

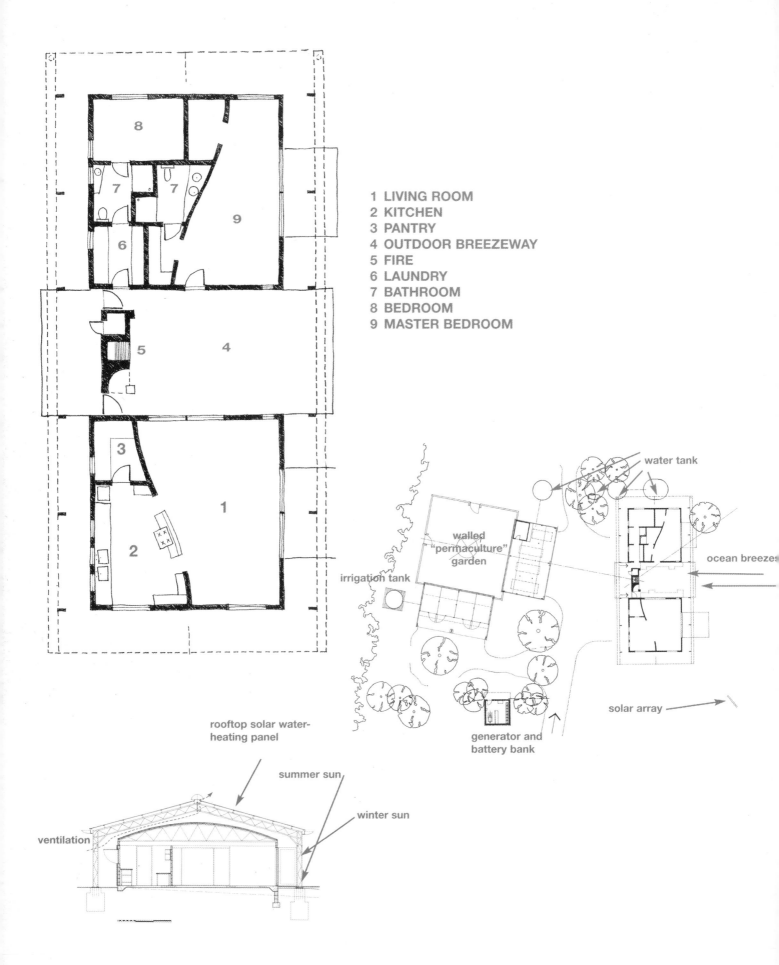

1 LIVING ROOM
2 KITCHEN
3 PANTRY
4 OUTDOOR BREEZEWAY
5 FIRE
6 LAUNDRY
7 BATHROOM
8 BEDROOM
9 MASTER BEDROOM

water tank

walled "permaculture" garden

ocean breezes

irrigation tank

solar array

rooftop solar water-heating panel

generator and battery bank

summer sun

winter sun

ventilation

The end of the house clearly shows the double-roof system, which allows air to move between the enclosure of the house and the super-structure above, a technique that helps to keep the interior cool in a hot environment.

Projects at a Glance

Project	Architect / Designer	Location	Size (sq. ft.)	100% Off the Grid
EXTREME URBAN				
Reade Street Townhouse (page 110)	John Petrarca	New York City, New York, USA	6,000	
URBAN / SUBURBAN				
Solar Umbrella House (page 40)	Pugh and Scarpa Architects and Engineers	Venice, California, USA	1,880	
D'Souza and de la Torre Residence (page 98)	Arkin / Tilt Architects	Belmont, California, USA	6,000	
House R128 (page 122)	Werner Sobek	Stuttgart, Germany	2,706	

Project	Architect / Designer	Location	Size (sq. ft.)	100% Off the Grid
RURAL (GRID INTERTIE)				
Barsotti Residence (page 54)	Arkin / Tilt Architects	Laytonville, California, USA	3,600	
Wilson Residence (page 132)	Breathe Architects	Mono Mills, Ontario, Canada	2,500	
RURAL (OFF THE GRID)				
Fargo and Maestas Residence (page 76)	Ryker / Nave Design	Clyde Park, Montana, USA	2,866	●
Twin Lakes Cabin (page 64)	David Buege	Minnesota, USA	620	●
Hill Country Jacal (page 88)	Lake / Flato Architects	Pipe Creek, Texas, USA	2,620	●
The Four Horizons Autonomous House (page 142)	Lindsay Johnston	Watagans National Park, New South Wales, Australia	2,620	●

Intertie	Backup	Water Collection	Geothermal	Solar	Wind	Solar Water Heater	Gray Water
•			•				
•	•			•			•
•				•		•	
•			•	•			

Intertie	Backup	Water Collection	Geothermal	Solar	Wind	Solar Water Heater	Gray Water
•	•			•		•	
•		•		•	•		•
	•	•		•	•		
		•				•	•
	•	•		•		•	•
	•	•		•		•	•

Resources

Architects, Designers, Builders, Technicians

Venice, California

Architect
Angela Brooks & Lawrence Scarpa
Pugh + Scarpa Architects and Engineers
Bergamot Station
2525 Michigan Avenue F1
Santa Monica, CA 90404
tel: (310) 828-0226 x 13
fax: (310) 453-9696

Designers
Angela Brooks, Lawrence Scarpa (principals) Ching Luk (project architect), Peter Borrego, Angela Brooks, Anne Burke, Michael Hannah, Vanessa Hardy, Anne Marie Kaufman Brunner, Fredrik Niilsen, Tim Peterson, Gwynne Pugh, Bill Sarnecky, Lawrence Scarpa (project design team)

Structural Engineer
Gwynne Pugh of Pugh + Scarpa Architects and Engineers

General Contractor
Angela Brooks and Lawrence Scarpa
Tom Hinerfeld of Hinerfeld Ward, Inc.
3734 Motor Avenue, Bldg. C
Los Angeles, CA 90034
tel: (310) 842-7929
fax: (310) 842-7934
www.hinerfeld-ward.com

Grid-Intertied Photovoltaic System
Source unavailable

Laytonville, California

Architect
Arkin / Tilt Architects, Ecological Planning & Design
1101 8th Street #180
Berkeley, CA 94710
tel: (510) 528-9830
fax: (510) 528-0206
www.arkintilt.com

General Contractor
Ken Gillespie
PO Box 1413
Laytonville, CA 95454
tel: (707) 984-7444
khg@direcway.com

Structural Engineer
Kevin Donahue / Toft deNevers & Lee
1101 8th Street, #180
Berkeley, CA 94710
tel: (510) 528-5394
fax: (510) 528-0206

Geotechnical Engineer
Busch Geotechnical Consultants
PO Box 222
Marcata, CA 95518
tel: (707) 822-7300

Deep Sand Bed Solar Space Heating System
Designer:
Bob Ramlow
Artha Renewable Energy
9784 County Road K
Amhearst, WI 54406
tel: (715) 824-3463
artha@wi-net.com

Installer:
Ken Gillespie
PO Box 1413
Laytonville, CA 95454
tel: (707) 984-7444
khg@direcway.com

Grid-Intertied Photovoltaic System
Joseph Marino
DC Power Systems
411 Matheson Street
Healdsburg, CA 95448
tel: (707) 433-1024
fax: (707) 433-5698
joepmarino@aol.com

TWIN LAKES CABIN	Twin Lakes, Minnesota
Designer	David Buege tel: (601) 354-6480 dbuege@sarc.msstate.edu
General Contractor	Matt Braaten Twin Lakes, Minnesota

FARGO / MAESTAS RESIDENCE	Clyde Park, Montana
Designer	Ryker / Nave Design 13 Cokedale Spur Road Livingston, MT 59047 tel: (406) 222-4788 www.rykernave.com
General Contractor	Ben Maestas, homeowner
General Carpentry and Framing	Jason Cipriani Cipriani Construction 1214 West Crawford Livingston, MT 59047 tel: (406) 223-0108 cell: (406) 222-4661
Photovoltaic & Wind System	Independent Power Systems, Inc. Tony Boniface 1404 Gold Avenue Bozeman, MT 59715 tel: (406) 587-5295

HILL COUNTRY JACAL	Pipe Creek, Texas
Architect	Lake / Flato Architects 311 3rd Street, Suite 200 San Antonio, TX 78205 tel: (210) 227-3335
Design Team	Ted Flato, principal Eric Buch, project architect
General Contractor	William Orr San Antonio, TX

D'SOUZA / DE LA TORRE RESIDENCE	Belmont, California
Architect	Arkin / Tilt Architects, Ecological Planning & Design 1101 8th Street #180 Berkeley, CA 94710 tel: (510) 528-9830 fax: (510) 528-0206 www.arkintilt.com
General Contractor	Danny Chan Contractor Ebcon Development Inc. 1506-D Dell Avenue Campbell, CA 95008 tel: (408) 378-1688 fax: (408) 378-8788
Construction Supervisor	Ray Baldhosky of Contractor Ebcon Development Inc.
Structural Engineer	Kevin Donahue / Toft deNevers & Lee 1101 8th Street, #180 Berkeley, CA 94710 tel: (510) 528-5394 fax: (510) 528-0206
Surveyor / Civil Engineer	Smith, Randlett, Foulk & Stock, Inc. PO Box 970 Redwood City, CA 94070 tel: (650) 368-1137

Deep Sand Bed Solar Space Heating System	Designer: Bob Ramlow Artha Renewable Energy 9784 County Road K Amhearst, WI 54406 tel: (715) 824-3463 artha@wi-net.com
	Installer: Jake Tornatsky Declination Solar 2245 Quesada Avenue San Francisco, CA 94124 tel: (415) 826-3985 jake@declinationsolar.com
Grid-Intertied Photovoltaic System	Installer: EcoEnergies, Inc. 171 Commercial Street Sunnyvale,CA 94086 tel: (866) SOL-WIND, (866) 765-9463, or (408) 746-3062 fax: (408) 746-3890 watts@ecoenergies.com
READE STREET TOWNHOUSE	New York City, New York
Architect	John L. Petrarca
General Contractor	Wildman & Bernhardt 102 West 38th Street New York, NY 10001 tel: (212) 714-1220
MEP Engineers (mechanical, electrical, plumbing)	Andrew Collins, PE 1140 Broadway New York, NY 10010 tel: (212) 696-5294
Structural Engineer	Hage Engineering 65 Bleeker Street New York, NY 10012 tel: (212) 358-7778
Geothermal Consultant	Carl Orio Water & Energy Systems Corp. 100 Maple Avenue Atkinson, NH 03811 tel: (603) 362-4666
Mechanical Contractor	PJM & Sons 1775 Broadway New York, NY 10019 tel: (212) 246-7671
Steel Fabricators	T2, Inc. 157 Oraton Street Newark, NJ 07104 tel: (973) 485-7600
Windows	Megawood by Windovations 2400 Vauxhall Road Union, NJ 07083 tel: (973) 313-0700
Insulated Concrete Forms	Reward Wall Systems 4115 South 87th Street Omaha, NE 68127 tel: (800) 468-6344

HOUSE R128	Stuttgart, Germany
Architect	Werner Sobek Ingenieure GmbH & Co. KG Albastrasse 14 70597 Stuttgart Germany tel: 49-711-76750-0 www.wsi-stuttgart.de
Energy System Design	Transsolar Energietechnik Curiestraße 2 70563 Stuttgart Germany tel: 49-711-67976-0
Heating / Ventilation / Plumbing Design	Hydraulics: Ing. Buro Muller Weissach
Control Systems	Baumgartner GmbH Westendstraße 19 77971 Kippenheim Germany tel: 49(0) 78 25 / 87 08 46 fax: 49(0) 78 25 / 87 08 47 info@baumgartner-gmbh.de
WILSON RESIDENCE	Mono Mills, Ontario
Architect	Martin Liefhebber + Associates, Breathe Architects 97 Simpson Avenue Toronto, ON Canada M4K 1A1 tel: (416) 469-0018
General Contractor	Colin Richards Kolapore Construction Inc. (Formerly C & R Contracting) tel: (905) 880-2732
Electrical	Phantom Electron Corporation 110 Ash Street, 2nd Floor Whitby, ON Canada L1N 4A9 tel: (905) 430-6512
Strawbale Construction	Camel's Back Construction c/o Chris Magwood RR #3, Madoc, ON Canada K0K 2K0
	Pete Mack / Tina Therrien PO Box 61 Warsaw, ON Canada K0L 3A0
Photovoltaic & Wind Turbine System	Bergey Wind Power Co. 2001 Priestley Avenue Norman, OK 73069 tel: (405) 364-4212
Structural	Read Jones Christofferson Ltd. 500 - 144 Front Street West Toronto, ON Canada M5J 2L7 tel: (416) 977-5335 x 500
FOUR HORIZONS AUTONOMOUS HOUSE	Watagans National Park, Australia
Architect	Lindsay Johnston 127 Seaforth Cresent Seaforth (Sydney) NSW 2092, Australia tel: 61 2 9907 8831
General Contractor	Lindsay and Su Johnston
Structural Engineer	Robert White
Solar / Wind Power Systems	Installed by Lindsay and Su Johnston

Dedication

To those individuals who are building great visions of a less resource-reliant life. May their mark be made in time, boldly and with lasting impression.

Acknowledgments

I would like to thank Gibbs Smith for his commitment to presenting a vision of how we may live in greater sympathy with the rest of the world, and for providing me the opportunity to participate in shaping this vision. Thanks to the staff at Gibbs Smith who helped guide me in the process along the way. Thanks to my editor, Johanna Buchert Smith, who helped answer many questions and believed in the project. Thanks to the people at Ryker / Nave Design who helped with feedback on direction of the book, especially Patricia Flores who took on many of the responsibilities for project coordination and graphic communication in the book. I would like to thank Brett Nave who was passionately building our new house through snow and heat wave while I sat quietly inside writing. Thanks to Montana State University School of Architecture and Clark Llewellyn who found ways to ease my academic burden while working on the book. Lastly, I would like to thank Tony Boniface, who over the past few years has helped me come to a better understanding of solar and wind energy.

Photo Credits

All photographs by Audrey Hall except:

Steve Brown: Page 142
Roland Halbe: Pages 122–131; 152, image d
Lindsay Johnston: Page 144; 148, upper
Michael Nicholson: Page 143; 145; 146; 147; 148, lower; 149, 151,
          153, image e

INDEX

OFF THE GRID